CHINA AFTER THE FIFTEENTH PARTY CONGRESS
New Initiatives

EAI Occasional Paper No. 1

CHINA AFTER THE FIFTEENTH PARTY CONGRESS
New Initiatives

EAST ASIAN INSTITUTE
National University of Singapore

Published by

World Scientific Publishing Co. Pte. Ltd.
P O Box 128, Farrer Road, Singapore 912805
USA office: Suite 1B, 1060 Main Street, River Edge, NJ 07661
UK office: 57 Shelton Street, Covent Garden, London WC2H 9HE
and
Singapore University Press Pte. Ltd.
Yusof Ishak House
National University of Singapore
10 Kent Ridge Crescent
Singapore 119260

CHINA AFTER THE FIFTEENTH PARTY CONGRESS: NEW INITIATIVES
EAI OCCASIONAL PAPER NO. 1

Copyright © 1997 by World Scientific Publishing Co. Pte. Ltd. and
Singapore University Press Pte. Ltd.

All rights reserved. This book, or parts thereof, may not be reproduced in any form or by any means, electronic or mechanical, including photocopying, recording or any information storage and retrieval system now known or to be invented, without written permission from the Publishers.

For photocopying of material in this volume, please pay a copying fee through the Copyright Clearance Center, Inc., 222 Rosewood Drive, Danvers, MA 01923, USA. In this case permission to photocopy is not required from the publishers.

ISBN 981-02-3364-7 (pbk)

Printed in Singapore.

FOREWORD

The East Asian Institute (EAI) is the successor of the former Institute of East Asian Political Economy (IEAPE). The mission of EAI is to promote research on East Asian development, particularly the political, economic and social development of contemporary China (including Hong Kong and Taiwan). In this regard, apart from publishing books, monographs and journal articles to cater to the academic community at large, EAI also prepares research reports on current developments in China and other parts of East Asia and makes them available to policy makers.

Our first three *EAI Background Briefs*, all dealing with events, comments and analyses related to China's recently concluded Fifteenth Party Congress, are put together as the **EAI Occasional Paper No. 1**, which should be of topical interest to readers who want to keep abreast of the latest developments in China.

October 1997 Professor Wang Gungwu
Director

CONTENTS

Foreword by Professor Wang Gungwu, Director of EAI   v

1. Good Political Arithmetick:
   China's Economy on the Eve of the Fifteenth Party
   Congress   1
   John WONG

2. Power to Set Own Agenda:
   Jiang Zemin's New Political Initiatives at China's
   Fifteenth Party Congress   21
   ZHENG Yongnian and ZOU Ziying

3. Reforming China's State-Owned Enterprises:
   Problems and Prospects   61
   John WONG and SIM Poh Kheng

List of Contributors   87

GOOD POLITICAL ARITHMETICK: CHINA'S ECONOMY ON THE EVE OF THE FIFTEENTH PARTY CONGRESS

John WONG

EXECUTIVE SUMMARY

1. China's economy on the eve of the 15th National Party Congress has again confounded observers with its highly creditable performance. Instead of the widely expected slowdown after its successful soft landing in 1996, it still turned in another robust growth of 9.5% for the first half of 1997, with inflation falling further to 1.6%.

2. What is most heartening to the present Chinese leadership is, however, the realization of its much-cherished price stability, a key precondition for social stability. With the retail price index (RPI) for July 1997 falling to 0.6%, China has clearly broken the backbone of its four-year long inflation with apparently no adverse trade-offs for lower output. Indeed, the Chinese economy may be heading for an era of sustainable high growth with low inflation.

3. Such a buoyant economic outlook on the eve of this crucial post-Deng Party meeting will naturally raise the political capital of Party secretary-general Jiang Zemin and win him support for his policy lines. A good "report card" on the economy also serves to legitimise the on-going reform progammes and embolden Jiang to take stronger reform initiatives.

4. All the pre-Congress clues suggest that the reform of state-owned enterprises (SOEs) will occupy the Congress's main economic agenda. Attention is currently focused on the Chinese way of privatization by converting SOEs into **shareholding cooperatives**. It remains to be seen if this scheme will be an effective instrument for Jiang to crack the SOE problem.

GOOD POLITICAL ARITHMETICK: CHINA'S ECONOMY ON THE EVE OF THE FIFTEENTH PARTY CONGRESS

John WONG[#]

Good Economics for Jiang's Politics

1.1 Economics, as a science, is about measurement involving numbers and figures. Among the early precursors of modern technical economics was an essay by a 17th century English philosopher Sir William Petty, entitled "Political Arithmetick", which was meant to be "the art of reasoning by figures upon things related to government...". As the Chinese Communist Party is to hold its 15th National Party Congress in the middle of this September, its secretary-general Jiang Zemin is certainly in need of some good "political arithmetick", not for governing China, but for him to maneuver his own agenda through this critical Party gathering. Jiang would want the Party to embrace his main policy lines for the post-Deng era and to endorse the selection of his younger protégés in key positions so as to lead China into the 21st century.[1]

[#] Professor John Wong is Research Director of the East Asian Institute. He is indebted to Miss Sim Poh Kheng, Research Officer, for preparing the tables and for some useful input to this paper.

[1] The first National Party Congress (NPC) was held in Shanghai in July 1921 to mark the formation of the Chinese Communist Party, attended by 12 delegates including

1.2 The Chinese economy, after its successful soft landing in 1996 with a 9.7% real growth and a much reduced inflation of 6.1%, has once again confounded foreign observers with its continuing high growth performance.[2] Instead of the expected slowdown for the first half of 1997, it still turned in another robust growth of 9.5% with inflation further falling to 1.8%. Strong economic fundamentals have led Chinese leaders to confidently predict that China's economy can possibly achieve 10% growth for the whole of 1997 with a minimal inflation.[3] Such a buoyant economic outlook will certainly boost Jiang's political capital on the eve of the Party Congress.

1.3 The external sector performance is even more impressive. Despite the general deterioration of the international economic environment, China's exports in the first seven months of 1997 registered 26% growth to US$96 billion while its imports grew by only 1.9% to US$76 billion, thereby yielding a substantial trade surplus of US$20 billion. This, along with a 15.6% increase in foreign direct investment to a total of US$26 billion in the same period, has contributed to the further

---

Mao Zedong and representing only about 50 Party members. The sixth NPC was held in Moscow in June 1928, representing about 57,000 Party members. The seventh NPC was held in Yanan in April 1945, representing some 210,000 Party members. After the establishment of the People's Republic in 1949, the first meeting was the eighth NPC, held in Beijing, representing about 10 million Party members. Since then, every NPC meeting has been eventful. The ninth NPC was held in 1969 amidst the Cultural Revolution; the tenth NPC in 1973 marked the downfall of Lin Biao; the eleventh NPC in 1977 was the first post-Mao meeting; ...the fourteenth NPC in 1992 was "post-Tiananmen", and the current fifteenth NPC is, clearly, "post-Deng". Since the eleventh NPC, after the death of Mao, the meeting has been held regularly once in five years. The present NPC represents a total Party membership of 58 million.
[2] See "Chinese 'miracle' confounds predictions", *International Herald Tribune,* July 23, 1997.
[3] The prediction was recently made by China's central bank governor Dai Xianglong. See "Nation sustains strong growth, low inflation", *China Daily,* August 15, 1997.

swelling of China's huge foreign reserves (currently hitting US$126 billion), and the stability of the *Renminbi*. Indeed, China's strong external financial balance presents a sharp contrast to the financial turmoil currently sweeping Southeast Asia. The Chinese leadership understandably takes considerable comfort for China's apparent immunity to such financial instability; but they also take the lesson of Thailand to heart.[4]

1.4 What is most heartening to the Chinese leadership on the economic front is not, however, China's success in sustaining high economic growth (a regular occurrence since the reform), but the realization of its much-cherished price stability, which is the key to overall social stability. It may be remembered that China's past high economic growth had also spawned double-digit rates of inflation. Vice Premier Zhu Rongji had to apply tough macroeconomic stabilization measures to cool the overheating economy. Now with the retail price index for July 1997 falling to 0.6%, Zhu has undoubtedly broken the backbone of the inflation. Even more significantly, Zhu has achieved this with apparently little adverse trade-off for lower economic growth (and hence the "soft landing"). Zhu's remarkable achievements in macroeconomic management have thus strengthened the Jiang-centred leadership, so much so that Zhu is slated to succeed Li Peng as China's next premier.[5]

---

[4] See "Will the Thai baht crisis affect China?", *Renmin Ribao* (People's Daily), Beijing, August 20, 1997. It is too early to judge if the current Asian currency crisis would render Chinese policy makers over-cautious in their planned financial liberalization process, which include the full convertibility of the *Renminbi* by 2000.
[5] For Zhu's achievement in inflation fighting, an American journalist has nicknamed him "China's inflation-taming 'Greenspan'". See *International Herald Tribune*, August 22, 1997.

1.5 With major economic troubles behind, Jiang can now turn his full attention to managing the politics of the 15th Party Congress. A national Party congress is usually an occasion for intense behind-the-scene politicking among different factions in order to exert their influence on high-level appointments (*Renshi-anpai* (人事安排) literally, "personnel arrangements") and on the Party's major policy lines. This is particularly the case for the upcoming 15th Party Congress, which is the first post-Deng meeting without the domination of a single strong man. Accordingly, Jiang has been sparing no efforts in mobilizing all his personal and institutional resources firstly, to extol the economic and social achievements of Deng Xiaoping's theory of building socialism with Chinese characteristics; secondly, to feature himself as the legitimate heir to Deng's main policy legacies; and thirdly, to use the label of "primary stage of socialism" to preempt leftist critique.[6]

1.6 In the run-up to the Party Congress, some Party ideologues brought back the old debate on the relative virtues of socialism and capitalism (the so-called 姓社或姓资 or "Mr. Socialist vs. Mr. Capitalist"). A motley group of leftists, conservatives and remnant Maoists have also exploited the dissatisfaction of the losers of the reform by mounting attacks on the central authorities for being responsible for undesirable "social contradictions" such as rising unemployment, including the widespread *Xia-gang* (下岗) phenomenon.[7]

---

[6] In recent weeks, the "People's Daily", the Party's main propaganda organ, has been carrying many articles and commentaries extolling Deng's economic reform and open-door policies, and China's past economic and social achievements since the reform, as well as Jiang's recent speech at the Central Party School on May 29, expounding the theme that China is now only at the transitional "primary stage of socialism". These documents are issued for Party cadres to study as their ideological preparation for the coming Party Congress.

[7] See, for example, "Jiang accuses leftist of exploiting anxieties", *South China Morning Post* (Hong Kong), July 31, 1997; and "The counter attack of Beijing's conservative group", *Ming Pao* (Hong Kong), August 15, 1997.

1.7 True, economic reform and the open-door policy have given rise to many negative social fall-outs, many of which are transitional in nature and can best be taken care of with continuing rapid economic growth in the longer run. Such is the basic rationale underpinning the government's present pro-growth strategies, which are unfortunately not shared by leftist detracters on ideological grounds. But in the short run, especially on the eve of this crucial Party Congress, China's continuing robust economic growth, as manifested in all these impressive economic numbers and statistics, can certainly strengthen Jiang's hands in countering the critics and doubters of economic reform. Few, of course, would expect such ideological attack on the central leadership, be it from the left or the right, to undermine Jiang's leadership.

1.8 More importantly, a good "report card" on the state of the Chinese economy, prior to the Party Congress, serves to legitimize the on-going reform programmes. This in turn would embolden Jiang to take stronger initiatives or even hard decisions for the next round of economic reform. Jiang is widely expected to put the reform of the state-owned enterprises (SOEs) at the centre of his economic agenda. The problems of SOEs are in fact well known to Chinese leadership, which has also realized that without accomplishing the reform of the state sector, the Chinese economy would continue to operate with all the well-known inefficiency of a partially reformed economy. But just how best or how effectively the new reform measures can be carried out remains to be seen. Jiang

---

"Xia Gang" is the retrenchment of redundant workers by state owned enterprises, and it has become a serious problem. According to the State Statistical Bureau, some 15 million workers have recently been made redundant by state-owned enterprises, representing 12.5% of the total urban labour force. Then there are rural surplus labour and the new entrants to the labour market ("Promising reemployment project", *Beijing Review*, August 18–24, 1997).

is presently preparing the political ground to push for the Chinese way of privatization by transforming many SOEs into "shareholding companies".[8]

Growth vs. Stability

2.1 The Chinese economy has been growing at about 10% since its economic reform in 1978 (Chart 1). Growth has been particularly spectacular for the past five years 1991–96, averaging at 12.1%. But such high growth gave rise to serious economic overheating, with inflation soaring to the record high of 27% in October 1994 (Chart 2). Since then, the restoration of price stability has been the government's top macroeconomic priority, which met its first success in 1996 when the economy "soft-landed" with 9.7% growth on the back of a moderate 6.1% inflation. Such a creditable soft landing is commonly attributable to Zhu Rongji's inflation-dampening austerity policy, which include price recontrol on essential food items and key commodities, drastic cutback in fixed capital investment and credit squeeze. Fortunately for China, the working of Zhu's macroeconomic stabilization measures was much facilitated by bumper agricultural harvests two years in a row and by the continuing influx of foreign direct investment. Hence Zhu was able to squeeze out inflation without squeezing output.

---

[8] The Party's Propaganda Department has recently requested cadres to seriously study Jiang's speech given at the Central Party School, in which Jiang called for the "third liberalization of thought, based on seeking truth from facts". The "first liberalization" was advocated by Deng Xiaoping in 1978 for a more open interpretation of Mao's thought in order to prepare China for the economic reform and open-door policy. The "second liberalization" was again advocated by Deng in January 1992 during his tour of South China, and Deng was asking people to put an end to the futile debate over "Socialism vs Capitalism" so that China could move forward to the "socialist market economy". This time, for the "third liberalization", Jiang is asking people to skip the debate over "public vs private ownership" so that he can push ahead for a fundamental reform of SOEs. See "Jiang promotes the third thought liberation of the Communist Party", *Xinbao* (*Hong Kong Economic Journal*), August 15, 1997.

Chart 1: CHINA'S ECONOMIC GROWTH AND FLUCTUATIONS (1979 - 1997)

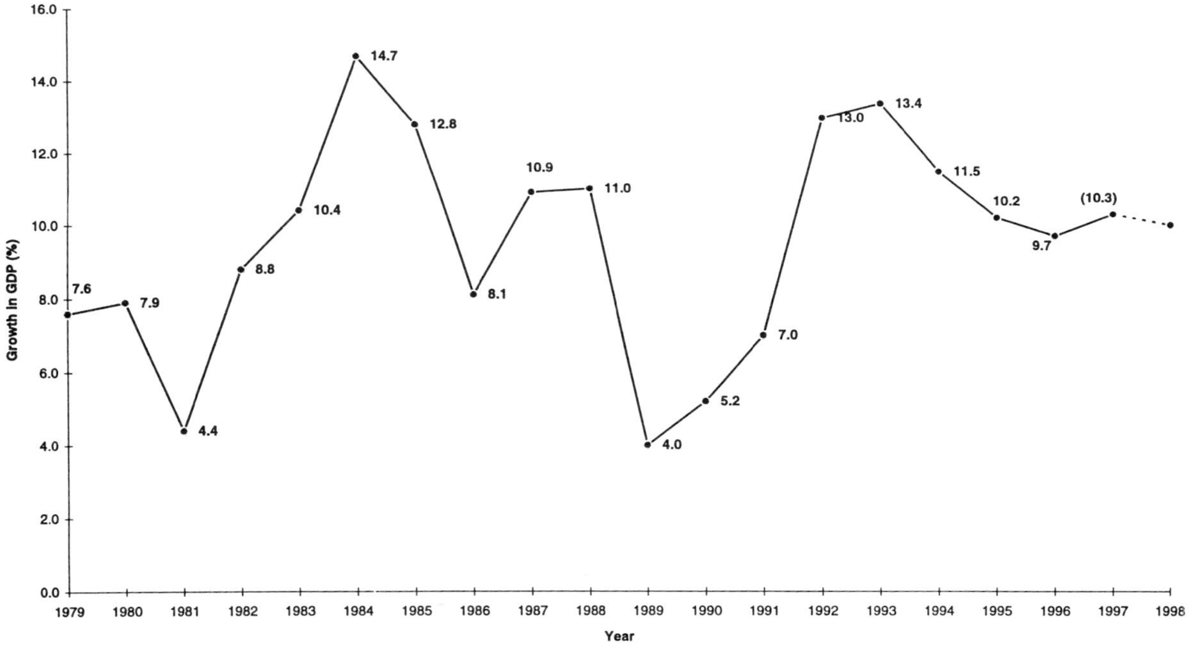

Year	Growth in GDP (%)
1979	7.6
1980	7.9
1981	4.4
1982	8.8
1983	10.4
1984	14.7
1985	12.8
1986	8.1
1987	10.9
1988	11.0
1989	4.0
1990	5.2
1991	7.0
1992	13.0
1993	13.4
1994	11.5
1995	10.2
1996	9.7
1997	(10.3)

Source: *State Statistical Bureau, Beijing*

Compiled by: *The East Asian Institute, NUS*

Chart 2: CHINA'S INFLATION 1994, 1995, 1996 AND 1997

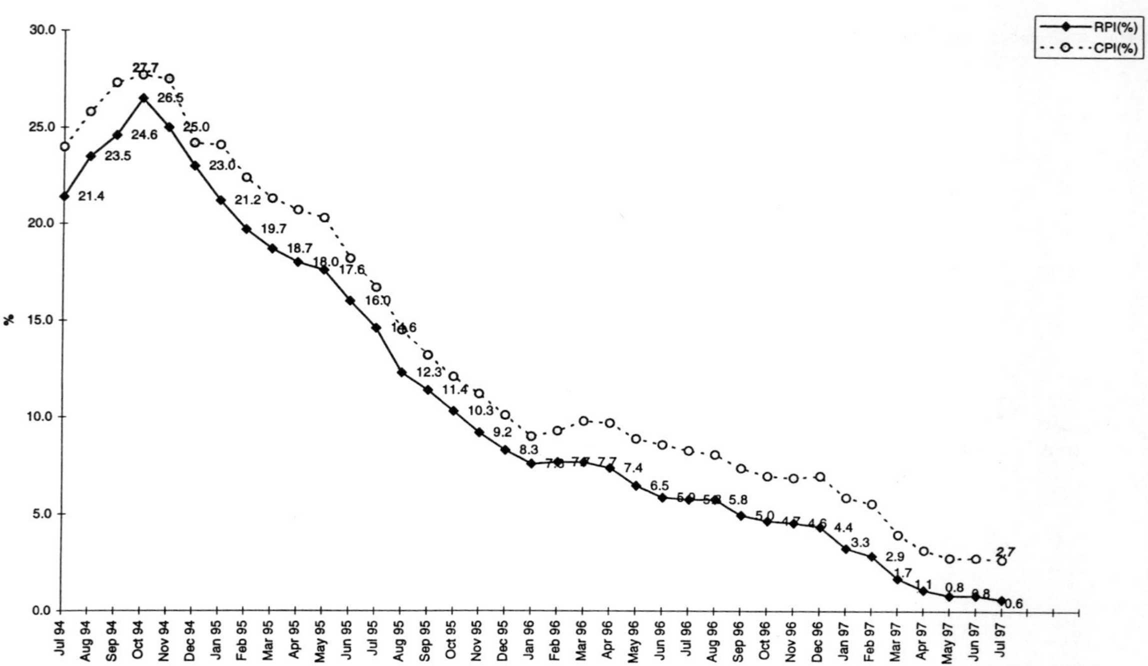

Source: *State Statistical Bureau, Beijing* Compiled by: *The East Asian Institute, NUS*

2.2 The Chinese economy entered 1997 on a distinctively deflationary note, especially for the first quarter. As inflation, measured by both retail price index (RPI) and consumer price index (CPI), continued to drift downward month by month, industrial growth also slowed down while both unemployment and stockpiling of unsold goods soared. Above all, the most significant growth-dampening factor has been the marked decline in the growth of fixed capital investment, which went down to 12% for the first sixth months of 1997 from the 1992 peak of 59%.[9] The Chinese economy at the beginning of 1997 was widely expected to slow its growth down to some "healthy" 8% in order to be compatible with the low inflation.

2.3 However, much to the surprise of many foreign observers, China actually posted a 9.5% growth for the first half of 1997 together with a very low inflation of 1.6% on RPI. As can be seen from Chart 3, the upturn occurred during the last two months of June and July, probably as a result of the loosening up of the tight monetary policy through two rounds of interest rate cuts, and corresponding increases in money supply (M2) and loans, at 19% and 18% respectively. Apart from increases in domestic demand, exports have also recovered, growing at 26% for the first seven months of 1997 (Chart 4).

2.4 Can there be some good "structural reasons" as to why the Chinese economy has achieved such impressive performance? Before Zhu Rongji, the Chinese government relied on blunt administrative means to fight inflation, often resulting in boom-bust cycles. Since 1993, Zhu has learned to apply a mixture of market-based instruments with some subtle administrative devices for appropriate macroeconomic controls. For instance, the People's Bank of China has put in place a more

---

[9] See "Macro controls anchor growth rate", *China Daily*, August 21, 1997.

Chart 3: CHINA'S MONTHLY INDUSTRIAL VALUE-ADDED 1996-1997

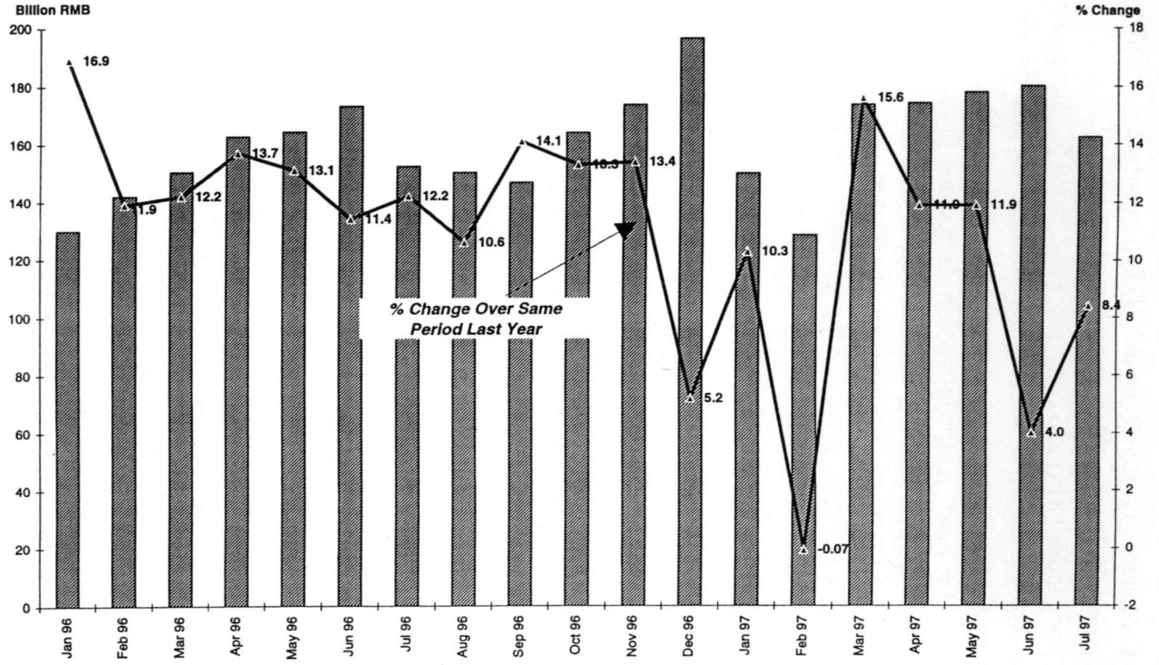

Source: State Statistical Bureau, Beijing

Compiled by: The East Asian Institute, NUS

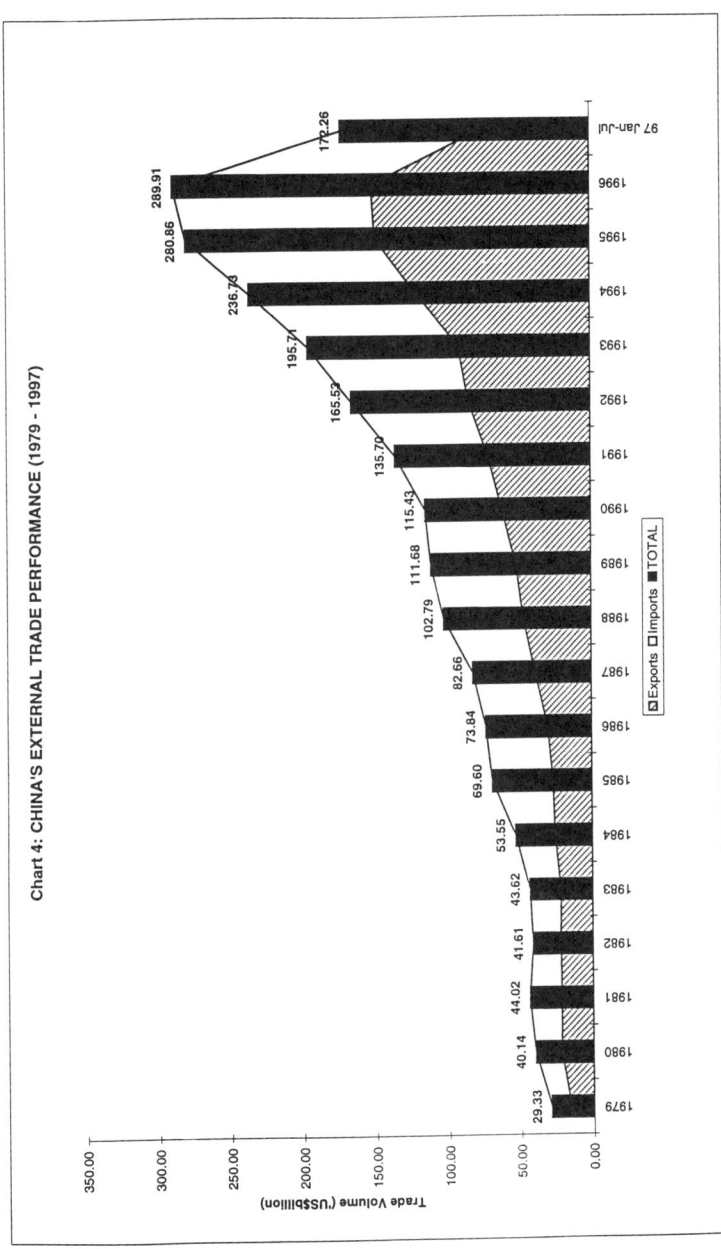

effective system for monitoring credit and loans at its local branches, thanks to its computerization efforts and related administrative reforms. In other words, China has been steadily perfecting its macroeconomic fine-tuning techniques in recent years. Accordingly, Zhu's increasing skill in macroeconomic management was paid off in the form of more favourable output-inflation trade-off technically, causing a shift of the traditional type of Phillips Curve towards the left. If this were true, the Chinese economy would be heading for an era of sustainable high growth with low inflation.

2.5 To be sure, there are no signs that the low inflation trend may be reversed in the second half of 1997. But it is far from certain that the high growth momentum will continue throughout 1997 as to end up in a 10% growth. Beijing has already revealed its preference for stability to growth, and the underlying political condition for such a preference is not likely to change so drastically as to justify a large measure of reflation after the 15th Party Congress, simply because further economic reforms would still call for a stable macroeconomic environment. However, China may find it increasingly difficult to sustain its present strong export growth (mainly driven by a sharp rise in the export of textile and garments) for the rest of 1997, because the recent depreciation of several Southeast Asian currencies could turn regional export comparative advantage against China, reversing the very force which used to favour China in the past few years over its competing Southeast Asian economies. All in all, there may be some uncertainty over China's economic growth in the second half of 1997; but it would not be serious enough to cause Jiang's leadership too much worry.

New Approach to the Old SOE Problem?

3.1 The immediate economic challenge for Jiang is actually how to put forth his own programmes of economic reform for endorsement by the Congress. Judged by pre-Congress speeches of top Party leaders, the reform of state-owned enterprises (SOEs) will occupy the Congress's main economic agenda. Indeed, the SOE reform is one crucial area which has so far not achieved any significant breakthrough.[10] This is because SOE reform is technically more complicated, and politically and socially more difficult to implement than any previous reform items. But China must thoroughly reform and restructure its SOE sector before it can complete its transition to a full "socialist market economy".[11] A simple bottom-line approach is to allow the many ailing SOEs to go bankrupt or to wait until a workable national social safety net is in place. Obviously, neither is a viable option for now. Thus, all eyes will be on the kind of new SOE reform strategy Jiang will unravel at the Congress—how much of it represents rhetoric, and how much is implementable substance.

---

[10] In 1978, SOEs accounted for 78% of China's total industrial output; but the figure declined sharply to only 31% by 1995. The relative decline of the SOE sector over the years may just reflect the dynamic expansion of the non-state sector, which includes township and village enterprises (TVEs) and various forms of individual and foreign-owned enterprises. Despite its relative shrinkage, the SOE sector remains large in terms of employment, fixed assets, and exports. In 1995, there were about 118,000 *industrial* SOEs, of which approximately 16,000 were considered "large and medium". They together provided 55% of total urban employment. Most SOEs are engaged in raw material and energy production as well as in heavy industry, including a wide range of capital-intensive industries that have to operate on the economies of scale. In fact, the bulk of China's basic industrial raw materials and intermediate products are produced by SOEs.

[11] As Premier Li Peng said during his recent visit to Singapore, "Not all SOEs are bad; and their problems have been exaggerated by foreign media". He is quite right in a way. China has compiled its own equivalent to the "Fortune 500", and most of them, including the annual top performers, are SOEs. So are those listed on the Hong Kong Stock Exchange as H shares, and more recently "Red Chips".

3.2 To crack the SOE problem, the Chinese government, to its credit, has actually been quite open-minded in experimenting with various reforming strategies. Prior to 1993, the reform focus was placed on improving enterprise governance such as greater managerial autonomy and greater accountability of enterprises. Over the years, progress in price reform has also provided a much improved external economic environment for SOEs to operate. In recent years, especially after the enactment of the new Company Law, the main emphasis has shifted to "corporatization" by encouraging SOEs to restructure into modern enterprise groups, or to convert themselves into "shareholding companies". Suffice it to say that the government will continue to attack the SOE problem on many fronts. In terms of the actual implementation strategy, the slogan in recent years has been *Zhua-da fang-xiao* (抓大放小) strategy, (concentrating on large SOEs and letting smaller ones go). In this regard, over 2,500 large and medium SOEs have been earmarked for trying out various ways of reform, half of which have been converted into "shareholding companies" while some have been formed into 57 modern enterprise groups (soon to increase to 120).[12]

However, the overall performance of the SOE sector has remained consistently weak, fundamentally because they still operate under some kind of "soft budget constraints". According to a report from the State Planning Commission, in the first part of 1997, some 46.8% of all SOEs reported losses, up 2.7% over the same period of last year.

Regardless of the real extent of the SOE losses and their real causes, China's SOE sector poses at least two serious problems to the Chinese economy: (1) an ailing SOE sector, controlling a disproportionately large share of physical and human resources, badly distorts the whole economy—clearly a classical case of misallocation of resources on a gigantic scale; and (2) the existence of an inefficient state sector has become an obstacle for the reform efforts of other sectors, particularly the financial sector reform. When large SOEs were making losses, the state banks would have to bail them out, leading to the accumulation of too many bad loans for the state banks—the official figure for non-performing loans in the state banks is 18%. And the problem of bad debt, in turn, hinders banking reform.

[12] "A review of SOE reform since the 14th Party Congress", *Renmin Ribao* (Beijing), August 28, 1997.

3.3 The pre-Congress debate on the SOE reform policy clearly points to a growing interest in the shareholding system, indicating that Jiang's new SOE reform strategy is likely to focus on the conversion of the majority of the SOEs into some kind of shareholding companies, particularly the so-called **shareholding co-operatives**. It is well known that a lot of SOE problems can be traced to their weak internal incentive mechanism associated with state ownership and control. Without owning a stake in the enterprise, workers and management do not have the inherent incentive to perform well. Thus, China started its first experimentation of a shareholding system as early as in 1983; but it was only after 1992 that more SOEs were converted into shareholding companies. China has by now over 9,000 formally registered shareholding companies, mostly small to medium in size. For the 1,000 or so large SOEs, the government has been reluctant to diversify its ownership by converting them into shareholding companies. But why such a renewed interest in the shareholding system this time?

3.4 From all the pre-Congress clues, Jiang's leadership has apparently taken the view that for the numerous small and medium SOEs, especially those controlled by local governments, privatization remains the most effective approach to tackle such thorny problems as incentive mechanism, property rights, and depoliticization of economic management.[13] But privatization must be tactfully promoted without openly running afoul of the open ideological taboo involving the controversy of *gong* (公) vs. *si* (私) (or public vs. private ownership). Hence the recent limelight on the "shareholding cooperative", which is considered quite similar to the "collectively owned" township and village enterprises (TVEs) in terms of combining capitalist mode of production with socialist (or collective) elements of ownership.

---

[13] See, for example, the Reuters dispatch "China's leaders look set to promote private enterprise", *Business Times* (Singapore), August 18, 1997.

Ideologically, the shareholding cooperative suits quite well the current label of "primary stage of socialism" for China, which is used by Jiang to rationalize his new reform initiatives.

3.5 The shareholding cooperative, if successful, would be destined to be the Chinese way of privatization. Not enough operational details are known yet as to how a typical shareholding cooperative is to be organized and how the scheme is to be promoted.[14] The government has to sort out a number of conceptual and empirical difficulties before it can be effectively used as one of the main instruments to attack China's "cross-century problem" of SOE reform.

3.6 Deng's eminent success in the first phase of economic reform owes a great deal to his flexibility and pragmatism, based on his celebrated "Two-Cat Theory"—"It does not matter if the cat is white or black, so long as it can catch mice". If Jiang had similar pragmatism and strong political will for the SOE reform, he would similarly have to declare, "It does not matter whether an enterprise belongs to the public or private sector, so long as it makes profits".

---

[14] An important question is how a shareholding company will value its assets and how it will divide up the shares for allotment among the state or local government, the enterprise's own employees, and the legal entities like banks, pension funds etc. Currently a lot of debate is on whether each worker is allowed to vote as one shareholder regardless of the number of shares he has, and whether his shares can be bought and sold on the secondary market.

Some legal scholars have also argued that a shareholding cooperative is "neither a horse nor a mule", as it displays a contradictory mixture of the capitalist element of shareholding with the socialist element of a cooperative. See, e.g., "Shareholding cooperatives are in urgent need of proper legal rulings", *Xinbao* (*Hong Kong Economic Journal*, August 30, 1997).

POWER TO SET OWN AGENDA: JIANG ZEMIN'S NEW POLITICAL INITIATIVES AT CHINA'S FIFTEENTH PARTY CONGRESS

ZHENG Yongnian and ZOU Ziying

EXECUTIVE SUMMARY

1. The 15th Party Congress of the Chinese Communist Party (CCP) was convened in Beijing from 12–18 September 1997. It is the last congress this century and the first without strong men. Can the Party's boss Jiang Zemin consolidate his power in the Party without Old Guards behind the scene? Can the Party be capable of leading the country into the 21st century?
2. With the passing of the old generation of revolutionaries, the Jiang-centred third generation of leadership is increasingly challenged by China's dramatic socio-economic changes. The leadership not only has to promote further economic growth. More importantly, it has to cope with enormous undesirable socio-political consequences, which have been used by the Leftists to attack the reform. In order to counter the Leftist's challenge, Jiang initiated an ideological campaign by calling for a third liberation of thought. Central to the third liberation is to reiterate Deng's "economic development priority" strategy and call for using all possible means to promote the country's economic development.
3. For Jiang, what is important is to establish a strong leadership to implement the Party's agenda for development. This led to a major personnel reshuffling at the Party Congress. With Qiao Shi out of the Politiburo, Jiang Zemin is now without major challenges from other top leaders. With General Liu Huaqing's departure from the Standing Committee of the Politburo, Jiang has secured the Party's control over the military. With Jiang's recruitment of his supporters into the leadership, the Jiang fortress has been fully reinforced.
4. With Zhu Rongji and Li Lanqing in the Standing Committee, the leadership has become more capable of promoting economic

growth. But what is significant is that with Qiao's departure, the Party has made progress in resolving the "exit" problem for Party elders. Also, with the recruitment of young figures into key Party organisations such as the Politburo, the Secretariat and the Central Committee, the Party is ready for the next century.

5. With economic growth and political stability as its highest priority, the Jiang leadership is not able to pay enough attention to political reforms, especially political democratisation. Nevertheless, pressures for political reform exist. Jiang cannot wait until social demands for democracy arise. Jiang reconciles demands for political reform and political stability by proposing to develop democracy within the Party, and the rule of law, and to consolidate grass-roots democracy.

6. Without the Old Guards being around, Jiang is probably powerful enough to initiate his own political agendas in an attempt to create a new era associated with Jiang's name. Nevertheless, whether Jiang will be capable of having his agenda realised still needs the test of time.

POWER TO SET OWN AGENDA: JIANG ZEMIN'S NEW POLITICAL INITIATIVES AT CHINA'S FIFTEENTH PARTY CONGRESS

ZHENG Yongnian and ZOU Ziying*

Expanding Power by Political Initiatives

1.1 Politics is about power, as Italy political thinker Niccolo Machiavelli argued.[1] For new leaders who are not able to find a new base of political legitimacy, engaging in politics is vital for their long term career. A man newly risen to power cannot acquire greater reputation than by discovering new rules and methods, as Machiavelli continued.

1.2 Jiang Zemin, the General Secretary of the Chinese Communist Party (CCP), is now in such a position. Using power to discover new

---
* Zheng Yongnian and Zou Ziying are Research Fellows of the East Asian Institute. The authors would like to thank Professors Wang Gungwu and John Wong for their constructive comments on the earlier versions of the paper. Thanks also goes to Mr. Wong Chee Kong, Research Officer, for his assistance.
[1] See Niccolo Machiavelli (1469–1527), *The Prince and The Discourses*. Translated by Luigi Ricci and Christian E. Detmond (New York: The Modern Library, n.d.). Also see Harold D. Lasswell, *Politics: Who Gets What, When, How* (New York: McGraw-Hill, 1936).

methods for the sake of his own power and for the sake of the Party's future is Jiang's major agenda at the 15th Party Congress of the CCP held from September 12 to 18 in Beijing.[2] In order to establish himself as a real core of the CCP power hierarchy, Jiang Zemin has to take political initiatives to build new institutions and rules that belong to his age and in which the Party and the country can be effectively governed. In modern democracies, regular elections provide politicians with opportunities to initiate new political and economic agendas, as Joseph A. Schumpeter argued.[3] In China, without such elections, the Party congress becomes the most important institutional means for politicians to compete for power.[4] The 15th Congress of the CCP gives Jiang Zemin an opportunity to set forth his own agenda for China's development on his own initiatives.

1.3 It seems that Jiang Zemin never lacks the political will or initiative to seek and consolidate power for his own sake or for the sake of a Jiang-centred third generation of leadership. When Jiang came to Zhongnanhai, China's "White House", in the aftermath of the 1989 Tiananmen Incident, he attempted to keep a balance between conservatives and reformists even though he was promoted by Deng Xiaoping. For a newcomer unfamiliar with Beijing politics, Jiang's

---

[2] For a full text of Jiang Zemin's report delivered at the 15th National Congress of the Communist Party of China on September 12, 1997, see, "Hold high the great banner of Deng Xiaoping theory for an all-round advancement of the cause of building socialism with Chinese characteristics to the 21st century", *China Daily*, September 23, 1997.

[3] Joseph A. Schumpeter, *Capitalism, Socialism and Democracy*, 2nd. (New York: Harper, 1947), p. 269.

[4] Since its establishment in 1921, the CCP has survived 76 years. Almost all what the CCP called historical turning points occurred at the Party congresses. Through the Seventh Party Congress held in 1945 in Yanan, Mao Zedong established himself as the core of the CCP. It was the 12th Congress that enabled Deng Xiaoping to initiate various new institutions and rules for the Party and thus set the discourse of China's development.

moderate political line without doubt gave him a chance to learn to survive power politics. Nevertheless, with such a moderate line, Jiang tended to be rather conservative. China's political reform lost momentum after 1989. At one time, even Deng Xiaoping implicitly expressed his dissatisfaction with his new heir.[5] However, after Deng Xiaoping's high profile tour in South China, Jiang did not find any difficulties following Deng's call to push economic reform further. In the 14th Party Congress (1992), with strong support from Deng, Jiang was successful in establishing the "market economy" as the backbone of the CCP's ideology. By following closely Deng's reformist line, Jiang secured his position as the legitimate heir and defeated his challengers such as the Yang brothers.[6] Without doubt, the 14th Party Congress was a turning point for Jiang's political career. Jiang would not have consolidated his power without various political initiatives he took before and after the 14th congress.

1.4 Now comes the 15th Party Congress. What is different from the last Congress is that this time Jiang has been able to set forth his own agenda without pressures from elders. Victory belonged to Jiang at the 14th Congress because he won over the support of senior leaders such as Deng Xiaoping. With the passing of Deng Xiaoping, Chen Yun, Peng Zhen and other senior leaders, Jiang is now in a position

---

[5] Wu Guoguang, *Zhulu shiwuda* (Power Game in China), Hong Kong: The Pacific Century Institute, 1997, p. 20.

[6] Before Deng Xiaoping's tour in South China, Jiang turned to become rather conservative. Without political dynamism from high authorities, China's reform lost its momentum. Jiang's position was challenged by reform-minded political figures such as the Yang brothers, Yang Shangkun and Yang Baibing. But right after Deng's tour, Jiang made a U-turn and proposed rather radical economic reform policies. In the 14th Party Congress, with Deng's support, Jiang secured his position as Deng's heir with both conservatives such as Song Ping and Yao Yilin and the Yang brothers removed from the political bureau.

of independence and autonomy. Jiang was appointed by senior leaders as the core of the third generation of leadership at the 14th Congress. Without these senior leaders, the 15th Party Congress became a turning point for Jiang to secure his power position.

1.5 More importantly, the 15th Congress became a test to see whether Jiang can initiate new institutions and rules to govern the country and thus create a new era associated with Jiang's name and his leadership like what Mao Zedong and Deng Xiaoping did before. Certainly, this congress is important for both Jiang Zemin himself and the Party. It is the last Party gathering this century. The next Party congress will be in 2002. Throughout Chinese history, great emperors or political leaders never gave up their efforts to be crowned with eternal glory (名垂青史) either for themselves or for the country. For Jiang Zemin who loves to quote great names and celebrated dictums in history (名人名言), it is imperative to exploit the 15th Party Congress in order to gain a position for himself and for his leadership in Chinese history. Whether Jiang will be able to achieve such a glorious goal depends on at least the following three factors which became the major political agenda of the 15th Party Congress.

1.6 First, differing from the last Party congress, this time Jiang has to establish himself firmly as the core of the third generation of leadership without strong support from senior leaders. Second, from the Party's point of view, Jiang's task is far beyond simply consolidating a Jiang-centred leadership. More importantly, the 15th Party Congress has to deal with the issue of the next generation of leadership, i.e., the fourth, or even fifth generation of leadership. Without modern mechanism such as elections, the Party gathering becomes crucial in dealing with leadership succession (接班问题). Unlimited power struggle hurts the Party and brings chaos to the country. Institutionally,

Jiang has now already become the most powerful figure in the Chinese power hierarchy since Mao Zedong. Without doubt, how Jiang plans to transfer his power to his successor(s) is significant for both the Party and the country.

1.7 Most importantly, Jiang has to show that his leadership is capable of leading China into the 21st century. For the first three quarters of the 20th century, China was a turbulent country filled with revolution and power struggle. Deng Xiaoping ended China's century-long chaos. Nevertheless, Deng's reforms have also resulted in dramatic changes. The country indeed needs a new framework and new institutions to accommodate such drastic changes. It is certainly important for Jiang to convince the Chinese people that his leadership is capable of meeting China's domestic and international challenges and bringing a bright future to the country.[7]

Let Deng's Flag Fly: Ideological Restructuring

2.1 To be proficient at letters (文韜) was a necessary virtue for good emperorship in Chinese history. This heritage continued even after the CCP came to power in 1949. It was believed that the fact that Mao Zedong became the most powerful figure in the CCP was attributed

---

[7] The significance of the 15th Party Congress can be seen from a series of articles and commentaries recently published by *People's Daily*, the organ of the CCP. Before the 15th Party Congress, the Party initiated a propaganda campaign to popularise the Party's reform efforts and future reform lines (改革路线). See *Renmin Ribao* (*People's Daily*), August 5, 1997 and after. One author comments, a hundred years ago when the time of cross-century came to China, the country was in the shadow of humiliation imposed by Western powers. Now, this time everything is different. The new leadership is leading the country into a promising century, with no more humiliation, and no more "Opium War". See Jiang Xia, "Kua shiji de shike" ("A Time of Cross-century"), *Renmin Ribao* (People's Daily), August 13, 1997.

to his capability of theorising. Mao indeed emphasised that the CCP's major leaders have to be the Party's ideological and theoretical authority (理论权威). In effect, ideology has been the most crucial ingredient of the CCP's survival. As Franz Schurmann argued, ideology plays the role of glue that sticks different organisational parts of the CCP together.[8]

2.2 Owing to such unique functions, ideological restructuring is always given the highest priority by the Party congress, especially during the period of power succession. Deng Xiaoping restructured the Communist ideology and transformed the Party from a revolutionary and radical one to a reform-oriented and pragmatic one. By initiating a campaign of the so-called "first liberation of thought" after he came to power in the late 1970s, Deng established a non-Maoist reform ideology and provided an ideological legitimacy for his own reform agenda. In the 13th Party Congress in 1987, Zhao Ziyang proposed the theory of the primary stage of socialism in an attempt to provide a new ideological base for China's development. Similarly, during the 14th Party Congress, following Deng's call for a "second liberation of thought", Jiang Zemin established the theory of "socialist market economy" as the core of the CCP ideology.

2.3 When the 15th Party Congress came, Jiang encountered a situation similar to what Deng faced before. For Deng, it was an age without Mao. For Jiang, it is an age without Deng. What should be done? Should Jiang treat Deng like what Deng did to Mao Zedong? Without Deng,

---

[8] Franz Schurmann, *Ideology and Organisation in Communist China* (Berkeley and Los Angeles, University of California Press, 1968). As a matter of fact, ideology plays a complicated role in any political system. It can be used to justify and to preserve the status quo, or it can be utilised to transcend and transform the status quo (See Karl Mannheim's classic, *Ideology and Utopia: An Introduction to the Sociology of*

Jiang could reasonably establish himself as a theoretical authority within the CCP. Before the 15th Party gathering, the CCP initiated a so-called "third liberation of thought". Central to this wave of liberation is to "let Deng's flag fly" and re-affirm the "theory of primary stage of socialism". In the 13th Party congress, Zhao proposed the primary stage theory, aiming to defend his reform policies and rationalize various "negative" consequences resulting from these reform policies. But with Zhao out of power, the 14th Party Congress no longer mentioned the theory of the "primary stage of socialism." Now, this theory has come back again. What is Jiang's rationale in re-emphasising this theory?

Response to the Leftists' Challenges

2.4 What happened is that Jiang encountered serious ideological challenges from the Leftists. Without doubt, China's rapid economic growth has brought about enormous social problems. For the Leftists such as Deng Liqun and other old ideologues, these newly emerged problems were related to Deng's development strategy of "giving priority to economic development". To cure these diseases, Deng's reform line has to be modified somehow. Otherwise, the Party-state would be threatened. What do the Leftists worry about China's future?

2.5 The first issue that worries the Leftists is about the strategy of decentralisation and its negative impact on state capacity. Chinese

Knowledge, New York: Harcourt Brace Jovanovich, 1936). In China, with the lack of many effective modern political institutions, ideology has its unique functions. Ideology is the very foundation of the political legitimacy of government structure and authority. It is also an instrument for the exercise of power and the implementation of policy. Ideology can be used to persuade people to believe the legitimate nature of political power on one hand, and, on the other hand, force party cadres and government officials to identify with the top leadership, orient their behaviour and prevent their deviation from the central leadership's policy priorities.

economic reform is characterised by decentralisation. The national government decentralised different aspects of economic decision-making power such as fiscal and financial power, property rights and material allocation power to local governments at different levels, individual enterprises, even individuals, in an attempt to provide them with economic incentives to promote the country's economic growth. As a result, the local economy boomed, but the national government lost its capacity to co-ordinate local economic activities and balance regional development. Income disparities among different social groups and among regions were widened. For the Leftists, the rise of localism (地方坐大), ethnic nationalism, widening income disparities and so on are just some early signs of national disintegration. Therefore, if this direction cannot be reversed, not only the Party, but the whole country as well will be in trouble.

2.6 Second, it seems to the Leftists that the rise of middle-class has increasingly become a major threat to the CCP's dominant rule. With enormous difficulties in reforming the state sector, the central government encouraged the development of different non-state sectors such as collectives, joint ventures and private enterprises of various forms. Owing to such a policy, dramatic changes occurred. In terms of economic components (经济成份), the state sector is now no longer dominant.[9] The rapid development of the non-state sector seems irreversible. A booming non-state sector in China's coastal provinces such as Guangdong, Zhejiang, Jiangsu and Shandong is already well

---

[9] The gross value of industrial production from the state sector declined from 78.5 percent of the total in 1979 to 30.9 percent in 1995, while that from the collective sector increased from 21.5 percent to 42.8 percent during the same period. Also, as of 1995, the private sector produced 13.2 percent of China's total industrial production while foreign and other forms of enterprises produced 13.1 percent. Lawrence J. Lau, "Gain without pain: Why economic reform in China worked?", Public Lecture, East Asian Institute, National University of Singapore, July 22, p. 7.

known. However, even in China's industrial centre—the Northeast region, provincial government officials already attributed the slow growth of local economy to a dominant state sector. They thus have called for opening a "second front" to revive local economies. That means to make great efforts to introduce various forms of private economic activities.

2.7 What do these changes imply for China's political order? Old Leftists were afraid that a shrinking state sector would change the socialist nature of the CCP regime and the bourgeoisie and its representatives will take over political power.[10]

2.8 For the New Leftists,[11] the rise of middle class means something else. They are afraid that the CCP regime is likely to become an ultra-

---

[10] According to a widely circulated *Wan Yan Shu* (万言书 or literally 10,000 word letter),

> An economy of state-ownership is the pillar of the Chinese state. State-enterprises are where China's industrial workers locate and the sources of national revenues. The shrinking of state-enterprises will necessarily lead to the weakening of the Party's leading position and the decline of central power and capacity to cope with various issues, and thus impose a serious threat to the CCP regime. [Moreover], a rising private sector is increasingly becoming the backup force of a newly emerging bourgeoisie and their political demands. Historically, the rise of European bourgeoisie won in their struggle for political power based on their principle of "without representatives, without taxes" (无代表, 不纳税). Now, representatives of Chinese bourgeois also began to "buy" through "taxation mechanism," and "public goods" from the government such as the rule of law, order, national defence and even democracy.

See *Wan Yan Shu* (10,000 word letter), "Yingxiang woguo guojia anquan de ruogan yinsu" ("Some Elements that Influence our National Security," in *Yazhou zhoukan* (Asian Weekly), Hong Kong, January 14, 1996, p. 23.

[11] The term of the "New Left" was given by many Chinese commentators in mainland and Hong Kong. See *Yazhou zhoukan* (Asia Weekly), Hong Kong, September 18,

rightist one. Their reasoning is like this: because economic growth in China was achieved by privatisation, economic reform had resulted in a strong bureaucratic bourgeoisie. Without privatisation of state-owned enterprises, the private sector in China is still rather small. More importantly, rapid development of the non-state sector, including the collectives, are closely related to the "loss of state properties." This means that government officials often become entrepreneurs and privatise state properties. *Guanshang* (官商 or literally official-businessmen) has been a major driving force behind China's rapid growth. The CCP regime depends increasingly on such a bureaucratic bourgeoisie. Such a regime will not be capable of re-distributing income among different social groups and regions and will become more coercive toward its people.

2.9 How can this tendency be reversed? The New Leftists have become very nostalgic. They appealed to Maoism and called for their own versions of economic and political democracy. For them, economic democracy means that the government needs an egalitarianism-oriented distribution policy which will constrain the regime's ultra-Rightist tendency. Furthermore, political democracy can be achieved through institutionalising Maoist "mass democracy". Without mass participation in the political process, the people will not be able to share the fruits of development and their interests will be ignored by the regime.[12]

1994, pp. 26–7; and *Dangdai yuekan* (Current Affairs Monthly), Hong Kong, November 15, 1994, pp. 26–30.

[12] For example, see Cui Zhiyuan, "Mao Zedong 'wenge' lilun de deshi yu 'xiandaixing' de chongjian" ("Mao Zedong's idea of Cultural Revolution and the restructuring of Chinese modernity"), *Hong Kong Journal of Social Sciences*, No. 7 (Spring 1996), pp. 49–74.

2.10 Third, the Leftists are also worried about the impact of socio-economic changes on the CCP's ideology. No one doubts that the old ideology is no longer effective in constraining and regulating government officials' behaviour, let alone people's behaviour. But a new ideology has not come into being yet. Much confusion has arose. In the Leftists' words again, "What was regarded right in the past is now regarded wrong; what was regarded wrong in the past is now regarded right".[13] For the Old Leftists, it is a rising middle class that invalidates the Communist ideology. Many Party cadres and government officials at different levels as well as intellectuals now publicly proposed that China give up its state-ownership and accept private ownership. Indeed, they have been a driving force that is leading the country to capitalism. More important, the CCP regime is undergoing change. Now, more and more local government positions are filled by those from the private sector. With enormous economic resource in hand, they are developing a non-communist ideology.

2.11 The concerns raised by the Old Leftists and New Leftists are not without reason. Indeed, because they raised many practical issues facing the country such as income disparities, worsening morale, money worship, laid-off of workers (下岗工人), social chaos, etc., they are very appealing to the people. It is in this sense that both the New Left and the Old Left could pose a serious threat to Jiang Zemin and his leadership. The new leadership cannot totally ignore these issues. Otherwise, it will lose its ideological authority and thus the ideological base of its political legitimacy. It is against this background that Jiang Zemin re-emphasised the theory of the primary stage of socialism.

---

[13] *Wan Yan Shu*, "Yingxiang woguo guojia anquan," *op. cit.*, p. 26.

A Third Liberation of Thought?

2.12 Jiang Zemin certainly sees the need to fend off the Leftists' attack on Deng's reform policies. However, what Jiang wants is not simply to defend "Deng's flag." More importantly, Jiang has to establish himself as the Party's new theoretical authority. If Jiang Zemin is not able to defend himself and set forth his own theory of governing the country like what Mao and Deng did before, his position in the Party's hierarchy will be challenged.

2.13 Therefore, Jiang proposed "a third liberation of thought" before the 15th Party Congress.[14] On May 29, 1997, Jiang gave a talk at the Central Party School and set the tone of the 15th Party Congress, with the presence of all major central and provincial leaders.[15] After that talk, the CCP's propaganda machinery initiated a campaign to popularise the theme of the third liberation of thought in an attempt to create a favourable atmosphere for Jiang to be a theoretical authority.[16]

2.14 The meaning implicit in Jiang's re-emphasis on the theory of the primary stage of socialism is multifold.[17] First of all, it is understandable that Jiang wants "Deng's flag" to fly. As the heir to Deng Xiaoping, Jiang's political legitimacy is based on Deng's legacies.

---

[14] Ren Huiwen, "Jiang Zemin tuidong zhonggong disanci sixiang jiefang yundong" ("Jiang Zemin promoted the third liberation of thought of the CCP"), *Xinbao* (*Hong Kong Economic Journal*), August 15, 1997; also see *Ming Pao*, "The propaganda department of the CCP called for the third liberation of thought," August 12, 1997.
[15] Jiang Zemin's talk, see *People's Daily*, May 30, 1997.
[16] Ren Huiwen, "Zhonggong cong lilun shang weihu Jiang hexin quanwei" ("The CCP defends Jiang's authority as the core from the theoretical point of view"), *Xinbao*, August 22, 1997.
[17] On the economic side, see John Wong, "Good political arithmetic: China's economy on the eve of the fifteenth party congress," *EAI Background Brief* No. 1, East Asian Institute, National University of Singapore, 2 September 1997.

If Jiang tolerated the Leftists' attack on Deng's reform line, his own position would certainly be destabilised. This is also true to the third generation of collective leadership which was indeed put together by Deng Xiaoping. Facing challenges from the Leftists, Jiang and his leadership did not have any choice, but to strike back.

2.15 Second, even though Deng's reform line has resulted in enormous "negative" socio-economic consequences, China's rapid economic growth without doubt is attributed to Deng's reform. With no revolutionary experience, the new leadership is increasingly dependent on economic development for their political legitimacy. If economic reform made China chaotic, then the new leadership had to show that it was only a transitional phenomenon. It is in this context that Jiang reiterated the theory of "primary stage of socialism". In doing so, Jiang attempts to show that economic development is still the Party's highest priority. Since China is still on a primary stage of socialism, its main task is growth regardless whether it is socialistic or capitalistic. Meanwhile Jiang also wants to give an explanation to China's chaotic phenomenon. Because of the primary stage, the Party needs to allow so-called "negative" elements to occur. They are not inevitable. With the discovery of new institutions and methods, they can be controlled by the Party-state.

2.16 Third, by calling for a third liberation of thought, Jiang began to pursue his own way of ideological reconstruction. Yes, Jiang was the heir of Deng Xiaoping and it was necessary to defend Deng. But "let Deng's flag fly" is not the only purpose of Jiang's call for a third liberation. With the passing of Deng and other elders and with no more support from them, Jiang certainly needs to expand and consolidate his own power. This situation was similar to what Deng Xiaoping did to Mao Zedong. Deng did not totally abandon Mao's legacies. Deng took the political initiative and established his own theory of Chinese development. Now it is Jiang's turn. Indeed, as one scholar observed, after the 14th Party Congress, Jiang began to make efforts to formulate his way of governing the country, a way that is different from Deng's. While Deng consistently insisted upon decentralisation, Jiang put much emphasis on re-centralisation.[18] A new and a third liberation of thought is necessary for Jiang to develop a non-Deng theory. There is no contradiction between "letting Deng's flag fly" and "developing a non-Deng theory". For Jiang and his leadership, to continue to insist on Deng's theory is to develop and even to go beyond Deng's theory in accordance with changing internal and external circumstances.

2.17 In the early 1990s when the former Soviet Union and East European Communism collapsed, Deng initiated the second liberation of thought and argued that only by developing the country's economy and delivering economic benefits to its people, could the CCP survive the worsening international environment. The Chinese people were also appalled by socio-economic chaos occurring in these former communist states. This created a favourable condition for political stability. However, with these former communist states gradually recovering, the CCP is once again faced with both domestic and foreign challenges. How could the CCP regime continue to consolidate its political legitimacy to govern the country? Without doubt, a third liberation of thought can be regarded as a new call for the Party to pay attention to new conditions. For the people, it means that the regime is likely to do something new to economic and political reforms.

[18] Wu Guoguang, *Zhulu shiwuda, op. cit.*, pp. 20–23.

Strengthening the Jiang Fortress: Personnel Reshuffling

3.1 Mao Zedong once contended that after the political line was established, cadres became determinant. This is the Chinese way of policy implementation. China is still a country that lacks modern, rational institutions. In order to reach key decisions, there must be a core of the leadership. In order to have its policies implemented, the central leadership must choose those who are willing and have strong motivation to follow mandates from above.

3.2 During the Great Leap Forward movement and the Cultural Revolution, Mao eliminated almost all his foes and built a Mao fortress in order to implement his radical policies. Similarly, after Deng came to power, his first priority was to reform the system of Party and state leadership in order to have his reform programmes implemented.[19] As a result, radicals were ousted from party and state organisations and were replaced by younger and better educated ones. In terms of cadre system reform, the Deng era was called as an age of "technocracy".[20] Indeed, one of Deng's legacies was to transform the CCP as a revolutionary party to an administrative one. Local officials' economic performance became the most important standard for the central

---

[19] This was reflected in his most famous talk about political reform, see Deng Xiaoping, "On the reform of the system of party and state leadership" (August 18, 1980), in *Selected Works of Deng Xiaoping* (Beijing: The Foreign Language Press, 1984), pp. 302–325.

[20] See Lee Hong Yung, *From Revolutionary Cadres to Party Technocrats in Socialist China* (Berkeley: University of California Press, 1991); Cheng Li & Lynn White III., "The thirteenth central committee of the Chinese Communist Party: From mobilizers to managers", *Asian Survey* 28 (April 1988), pp. 371–99; Cheng Li & Lynn White III, "Elite Transformation and Modern Change in Mainland China and Taiwan: Empirical Data and the Theory of Technocracy", *China Quarterly* 121 (March 1990), pp. 1–39; Zang Xiaowei, "The fourteenth Central Committee of the CCP: Technocracy or political technocracy", *Asian Survey* 33 (August 1993), pp. 787–803.

leadership to judge their political achievements. At the top level, only those who showed strong support for Deng's reform policies could have access to power. More importantly, Deng used the Party's cadre system effectively to promote the country's economic modernisation.[21]

3.3 This is also true for Jiang. Jiang began to build his personnel fortress in 1992. Institutionally, Jiang took over power in 1992 when he was selected as the CCP's boss in the Fourteenth Party Congress. Through the 14th congress and its first plenum, Jiang established a Jiang-centred leadership and consolidated his relations with the military. In the Second Plenum in 1993, Jiang continued to emphasise organisational building of his power base. The Plenum endorsed the proposal of reforming the Party and government organs, aiming to improve the effectiveness of the Party-state's government. The focus of the Fourth Plenum in 1994 was still on strengthening party organisations. Major personnel changes were made in that session. Consequently, a Jiang-centred faction was firmly established, i.e., the Shanghai Clique.[22]

3.4 Nevertheless, Jiang is very cautious in dealing with different political factions at the top. Since the early 1990s, Jiang has been successful in winning support from the People's Liberation Army (PLA) and gaining co-operation from Li Peng, who has been in the top leadership longer than Jiang. However, when Jiang felt that his

---

[21] This has been called the "political logic of economic reform", see Susan L. Shirk, *The Political Logic of Economic Reform in China* (Berkeley: University of California Press, 1993).
[22] IEAPE Special Correspondent, "The decision of the Fourth Plenum—Coping with the decline of the Communist Party of China", *IEAPE Commentaries*, No. 10, 21 December 1994; and "The 4th Party Plenum—Emergence of a New Shanghai Clique in the Top Leadership", *IEAPE Commentaries*, No. 9, 18 October 1994.

leadership was challenged, he became determined. In 1995, Jiang reduced greatly the influence of the Beijing faction by removing Chen Xitong, who committed serious economic crimes, from the top leadership.

3.5 The 15th Party Congress without doubt reinforced the Jiang fortress by a major personnel reshuffling as shown in Tables 1 and 2. It is also obvious that Jiang continues to make efforts to consolidate his "Shanghai Clique" by bringing Zeng Qinghong into the Politburo (as an alternate number). It is important to note, however, that the "Jiang Fortress" is consolidated at this congress not only because the "Shanghai Clique" is expanded, but also because many of Jiang's supporters come from other areas. With many of experience at the centre of power, Jiang no longer needs to recruit his people exclusively from Shanghai. As shown in Table 2, newly recruited members of the Politburo were from different parts of China. Indeed, Jiang cannot be too openly ambitious in building his own fortress. Otherwise, he could be challenged by those whose power and interests are seriously threatened.

3.6 What is significant politically is the retirement of Qiao Shi and General Liu Huaqing. With Qiao Shi's retirement from all his posts in the CCP, Jiang is now without any possible challenger. More important, regardless of whether Qiao retired voluntarily or was forced to retire, his retirement is likely to resolve the "exit" problem endemic in the CCP. The "exit" problem has troubled the CCP and the country as well. When leaders become aged, they are not ready to give up their power positions. When young leaders "fight" in the front line, old guards stand behind them. Now with Qiao's departure, Jiang is setting up a procedure for old leaders to "exit" gracefully from their power positions when they become aged.

Table 1. Pre-15th Party Congress Politburo.

Name	Year of birth	Educational background	Power base
Jiang Zemin(江泽民)	1926	engineering	central and local
Li Peng(李鹏)	1928	engineering	central
Qiao Shi(乔石)	1924	social sciences	central
Zhu Rongji(朱镕基)	1928	engineering	central and local
Li Ruihuan(李瑞环)	1934	polytechnic	local
Liu Huaqing(刘华清)	1916	naval school	military
Hu Jintao(胡锦涛)	1942	engineering	local and central

\# above as members of the Standing Committee

Average age (years) **68.7**

Ding Guangen(丁关根)	1929	engineering	central
Tian Jiyun(田纪云)	1929	polytechnic	local and central
Li Lanqing(李岚清)	1932	business	local and central
Li Tieying(李铁映)	1936	physics	local and central
Yang Baibing(杨白冰)	1920	social sciences	military
Wu Bangguo(吴邦国)	1941	engineering	local
Zou Jiahua(邹家华)	1926	industrial management	central
Jiang Chunyun(姜春云)	1930	arts and social sciences	local
Qian Qichen(钱其琛)	1928	junior college	central
Wei Jianxing(尉健行)	1931	engineering	local and central
Huang Ju(黄菊)	1938	engineering	local
Xie Fei(谢非)	1932	(unclear)	local

\# above as members of the Politburo

| Wen Jiabao(温家宝) | 1942 | geology | local and central |
| Wang Hanbin(王汉斌) | 1925 | humanities | local and central |

\# above as members of the Politburo

Average age (years) **65.6**

Table 2. The New Politburo at 15th Party Congress.

Name	Year of birth	Educational background	Power base
Jiang Zemin(江泽民)	1926	engineering	central and local
Li Peng(李鹏)	1928	engineering	central
Zhu Rongji(朱镕基)	1928	engineering	central and local
Hu Jintao(胡锦涛)	1942	engineering	local and central
Li Ruihuan(李瑞环)	1934	polytechnic	local
Wei Jiangxin**(尉健行)	1931	engineering	local and central
Li Lanqing**(李岚清)	1932	business	local and central

above as members of the Standing Committee
Average age (years) **65.4**

Ding Guangen(丁关根)	1929	engineering	central
Tian Jiyun(田纪云)	1929	polytechnic	local and central
Li Changchun**(李长春)	1944	engineering	local and central
Li Tieying(李铁映)	1936	physics	local and central
Wu Bangguo(吴邦国)	1941	engineering	local
Wu Guangzheng**(吴官正)	1938	engineering	local
Chi Haotian**(迟浩田)	1929	military school	military
Zhang Wannian**(张万年)	1928	military school	military
Luo Gan**(罗干)	1935	engineering	local and central
Jiang Chunyun(姜春云)	1930	arts and social sciences	local
Jia Qinglin**(贾庆林)	1940	engineering	local
Qian Qichen(钱其琛)	1928	junior college	central
Huang Ju(黄菊)	1938	engineering	local
Wen Jiabao**(温家宝)	1942	geology	local and central
Xie Fei(谢非)	1932	(unclear)	local

above as members of the Politburo

Zeng Qinghong**(曾庆红)	1939	engineering	local
Wu Yi**(吴仪)	1938	engineering	central

above as members of the Politburo
Average age (years) **61.9**

** newly recruited member

3.7 With Liu Huaqing's departure from the Standing Committee, it seems that Jiang has secured his control over the military. But the significance of General Liu's departure is more than that. It is for the first time in the history of People's Republic that no representative from the military appears in the Standing Committee. In the pre-reform period, Mao Zedong controlled the military for more than 27 years (1949–1976), supported by Zhu De, Lin Biao, Ye Jianying and other generals. Deng Xiaoping was also capable of exerting the control over the military owing to his strong military background. When Zhao Ziying was General Secretary of the Party, there was no military representative in the Standing Committee. Nevertheless, it was Deng Xiaoping that controlled the military behind the scene. Now, among seven members of the Standing Committee, no one has military background. This implies that with the passing of old strong military men, the Party, not individual leaders, will control the gun. With the weakening of military presence at the top leadership, China's transition to a modern civil-military relationship is likely to occur in the near future.

3.8 Personnel reshuffling at this congress also shows that the top leadership has become determined to promote economic reform further. China's economic reform is approaching its most difficult part, i.e., the state-owned enterprise reform. The SOE reform is not only about economics; it is also about politics. Without the top leadership's determination and commitment, it is doubtful whether the Party will succeed in SOE reform. Fortunately, a consensus on economic reform seems to have been reached within the top leadership. Major leaders came to their positions because of their success stories of economic management either in the provinces or in central bureaucracies. With Zhu Rongji and Li Lanqing in charge of economic matters, the Party leadership obviously expressed its concern of "economic priority". Zhu has been known as China's economic czar. Since 1993, Zhu has been

Power to Set Own Agenda 45

successful in managing China's economic transition. Before the 15th Party Congress, Zhu promised to introduce dramatic changes to China's SOEs. Obviously, his determination was recognised by other major leaders. Consistent with Zhu's initiatives, Jiang has also emphasised that the Party will use all possible means to reform SOEs. So, even if disagreement is likely among top leaders, the consensus of economic reform remains.

3.9 But for Jiang Zemin and his leadership, the most important issue facing the 15th Party Congress is how a fourth and even a fifth generation of leadership can be established. With the passing of the Old Guards, Jiang and his third generation are now in charge of building the next generation of leadership. In previous Party gatherings, Old Guards such as Deng Xiaoping, Chen Yun, Ye Jianying and Li Xiannian were powerful enough to choose their own successors. However, even these powerful figures were not able to make sure that power succession could be smooth as shown in the cases of Hu Yaobang and Zhao Ziyang. Major leaders of the third generation have learned from China's past experience that power succession, especially in an age of great transformation, is vital both for the Party itself and for the country. Without the Old Guards, the Standing Committee of the Politburo as a whole had to play the role of guardians to choose the next generation of leadership.

3.10 As Table 2 shows, the Standing Committee still encounters the problem of ageing. By the next party congress (2002), the rest of committee members will be over 70, except Hu Jintao. Nevertheless, younger figures have been recruited into the Politburo, the Secretariat, and the Central Committee. Among 193 members of the Central Committee, about 52 percent were newly recruited. The new recruits are younger and better educated. Table 3 shows the age structure of the Central Committee. With the recruitment of new figures into these organisations, the next generation of leadership is expected to be ready by the next Party gathering in 2002.

Table 3. Age Structure of the Central Committee at the 15th Party Congress (344 Members and Alternate Members).

Age range	No.	Percentage
61 and above	68	619.8%
56–60	118	34.3%
51–55	107	31.1%
50 and below	51	14.8%

Source: *Renmin Ribao* (People's Daily), September 19, 1997.

3.11 More important are personnel changes at the provincial level. Deng Xiaoping was successful in promoting China's rapid economic growth mainly because he was able to have a group of reform-minded local party cadres and government officials. With Zhao Ziyang and Wan Li summoned to Beijing and with reformist local leaders coming into key positions, China's economic reform gained a political dynamism. Also because of the introduction of "new blood" into the central leadership from the provinces, the third generation has been able to present an energetic image. Jiang Zemin, Zhu Rongji, Hu Jintao and many others have benefited from their local experience, let alone other figures such as Wu Bangguo, Li Ruihuan, Jiang Chunyun and others. Now that the third generation has become the selector, it has to recruit those young figures who have been successful in managing local business into key provincial positions as an effort to build the fourth and fifth generation of leadership.

3.12 Prior to the 15th Party Congress, a major personnel reshuffling took place at the provincial level. Within less than one year, some 11 provinces had their new Party secretaries (see Table 4). This is not the place to give a detailed analysis of provincial personnel reshuffling. But some characteristics of the reshuffling merit notice. According to the China News Agency, this large scale personnel reshuffling took place in order to meet the Party's requirements of the new leadership, including provincial leaders' educational level, age and their experience in different locations.²³ Among 11 newly appointed provincial Party secretaries, six were born in the 1940s such as Jia Qinglin (Beijing), Wen Shizhen (Liaoning), Cao Bochun (Guangxi), Li Jianguo (Shanxi), Ling Huan (Yunnan) and Tian Chengping (Qinghai). Most new appointees received high education with sciences and engineering backgrounds. It is also worth noting that this provincial personnel reshuffling is also characterised by what the CCP called "personnel exchange" (人事交流), i.e., local leaders are transferred to different places. Obviously, "personnel exchange" is a legacy of the traditional "avoidance system" (回避制度) which Chinese emperors used to restrain localism. It has also become a legacy of the CCP. Mao used it to control Party cadres and government officials' behaviour. Deng Xiaoping used it even more skilfully. What Susan Shirk called "playing to the provinces" means that the central leadership uses its personnel system to control the rise of localism on one hand, and to provide local officials with greater political incentives to promote local economic growth on the other hand.²⁴ Jiang and his leadership has certainly played with this system to achieve what Deng did before. But for Jiang, the system can also be used to "dig out" potential candidates for the next generation of leadership. Predictably, many future top CCP leaders will be chosen from these local figures.

[23] *Hong Kong Economic Daily*, 2 September 1997, A29.
[24] Susan L. Shirk, *The Political Logic of Economic Reform in China* (Berkeley: University of California Press, 1993).

Table 4. Personnel Reshuffling at the Provincial Level.

Province	Party Secretary	Governor
Beijing	**Jia Qinglin**(贾庆林)	Jia Qinglin(贾庆林)
Tianjin	**Zhang Lichang**(张立昌)	Zhang Lichang(张立昌)
Hebei	Cheng Weigao(程维高)	Ye Liansong(叶连松)
Inner Mongolian	Liu Mingzu(刘明祖)	Wuliji(乌力吉)
Liaoning	**Wen Shizhen**(闻世震)	Wen Shizhen(闻世震)
Helongjiang	**Xu Youfang**(徐有芳)	Tian Fengshan(田凤山)
Jilin	Zhang Dejiang(张德江)	Wang Yunkun(王云坤)
Shanghai	Huang Ju(黄菊)	Xu Kuangdi(徐匡迪)
Jiansu	Chen Huanyou(陈焕友)	Zheng Silin(郑斯林)
Zhejiang	Li Zemin(李泽民)	Chai Songyue(柴松岳) (acting)
Anhui	Lu Rongjing(卢荣景)	Hui Liangyu(回良玉)
Fujian	Chen Minyi(陈明义)	He Guoqiang(贺国强)
Jianxi	**Shu Huiguo**(舒惠国)	Shu Shengyou(舒圣佑)
Shandong	**Wu Guanzhen**(吴官正)	Li Chunting(李春亭)
Henan	Li Changchun(李长春)	Ma Zhongchen(马忠臣)
Hubei	Jia Zhijie(贾志杰)	Jiang Zhuping(蒋祝平)
Hunan	Wang Maolin(王茂林)	Yang Zhengwu(杨正午)
Guangdong	Xie Fei(谢非)	Lu Ruihua(卢瑞华)
Guangxi	**Cao Bochun**(曹伯纯)	Cheng Kejie(成克杰)
Hainan	Ruan Chongwu(阮崇武)	Ruan Chongwu(阮崇武)
Sichuan	Xie Shijie(谢世杰)	Song Baorui(宋宝瑞)
Yunnan	**Ling Huan**(令狐安)	He Zhiqiang(和志强)
Guizhou	Liu Fangren(刘方仁)	Wu Yixia(吴亦侠)
Shannxi	**Li Jianguo**(李建国)	Chen Andong(程安东)
Gansu	Yan Haiwang(阎海旺)	Sun Ying(孙英) (acting)
Qinghai	**Tian Chengping**(田成平)	Bai Enpei(白恩培) (acting)
Ningxia	**Mao Rubai**(毛如柏)	Bai Lizhen(白立枕)
Xinjiang	Wang Lequan(王乐泉)	Abulahat Abdurixit (阿不来提·阿不都热西提)
Tibet	Chen Kuiyuan(陈奎元)	Gyaincain Norbu(江村罗布)
Chongqing	Zhang Delin(张德林)	Pu Haiqing(蒲海清)

\# Those in bold are newly appointed part secretaries.

Political Reform Implicit in Political Practice

4.1 As Chinese top leaders keep changing their perception of the importance of "economic priority," China's economy has grown dramatically. But the top leadership has been hesitant about its political reform. As shown in Table 5, major leaders have made progress in their consensus about China's economic reform. Even though reformist leaders' economic policies often come under attack by Leftists, some major new "economic theories" can finally be put forward by the top leadership. This is what happened to the Party congresses since the Deng era.

4.2 However, the situation is rather different on the political side. The difficulties of political reform are multifold. First, compared to economic reforms, political reforms are more about power redistribution among major leaders and different party-state organisations. While economic reforms often result in a win-win situation, political reforms can become a zero-sum game. Resistance to any forms of political reform can be strong from those who will possibly lose the battle. Second and more importantly, political reform is about power distribution between the Party-state and society. In other words, political reform necessarily means the democratisation of the country to some extent even though it is not real democracy. If democracy occurs, the whole political structure will change, and political stability will be in doubt and instability can damage the country's economy. Third, there is a structural difficulty in initiating the country's political reform. In a Leninist state, because everything is politicised by the Party-state, political reform will be impossible without initiatives from above. The Party-state must be powerful enough in order to initiate reform programs and have them implemented. That implies that political authoritarianism is a pre-condition for China's political reform. Authoritarianism, however, is contradictory with political reform, not to mention democratisation.

Table 5. Main Concepts Proposed by the Party Congresses.

Party Congress	Economic Reform	Political Reform
12th (1982)	Planned economy as the main pillar and market economy as a supplementary element	Recruiting young and professionals into the Party leadership; abolishing the lifelong office-holding system; reform the party and state system
13th (1987)	Combining planned and market economy theory of primary stage of socialism	Developing socialistic democracy; establishing and strengthening the grass-roots democracy; political participation
14th (1992)	Socialist market economy	Anti-corruption (no major concept of political reform was mentioned)
15th (1997)	Theory of primary stage of socialism; market economy; shareholding co-operatives and any other possible means to develop the economy	Anti-corruption; strengthening grass-roots democracy; the rule of law; "democratic supervision," etc.

4.3 This is what occurred to China since the Deng era. In the early 1980s, Deng Xiaoping argued that political reforms were necessary in order to promote economic reform and to protect the "fruits" resulting from economic reform. Changes were introduced to China's political system. The lifelong office-holding system (终身制) was eliminated. A young generation of leaders was recruited into the top leadership. Deng indeed encouraged political discussions among social and political groups in order to establish a new theoretical basis for a new era. He also allowed people to criticise the Party and the state to some extent. However, when criticism of the system *per se* came into being, Deng and his old generation of leadership became intolerant. What Deng Xiaoping needed was to improve the Party-state's performance by institutional reforms. From the 12th Party Congress (1982) to the 13th Party Congress, various political campaigns such as "anti-spiritual pollution" and "anti-bourgeois liberalisation" were initiated. In 1986, Hu Yaobang, then General Secretary, was forced to resign due to his ambiguous attitudes toward "bourgeois liberalisation".

4.4 During the 13th Party Congress, the Party's General Secretary Zhao Ziyang proposed a rather "radical" programme for China's political reform. With Deng's support, Zhao argued that a socialist democracy had to be developed in order to facilitate economic reform. According to Zhao, to promote democracy, the Party-state had to allow social forces to participate in politics. His programme included grassroots democracy and social supervision over government. Nevertheless, Zhao's program remained largely rhetorical. With the occurrence of the 1989 Tiananmen demonstration, Zhao's political reform came to an end.[25]

---

[25] On Zhao Ziyang's program of political reform at the 13th Party Congress, see Yan Huai, "Zhao Ziyang's bold political reform attempts at the 13th Party Congress", *IEAPE Background Brief* No. 67, 8 July 1994.

4.5 Because of China's own experience, and also because of chaos in the former Soviet Union and later Russia as a result of radical political reform, the 14th Party Congress (1992) no longer talked about political reform. With Deng's South tour, the whole country's attention overwhelmingly turned to economic activities or "下海" (literally, go to the sea of business). With enormous economic opportunities being open to the people, the pressure for political reform was decreased. Social and political forces were more geared to political stability and economic profits rather than political reform and democracy. The Party did mention political reform in the communiqué of its 14th Party Congress. But central to it was anti-corruption, not wider political participation.

4.6 However, this does not mean in any sense that political reform is not significant for China. With more than eight years in power, Jiang now understands why political reform is imperative for himself and for the Party. Various crucial problems need to be resolved through political reforms such as corruption among government officials, power succession or the selection of new leaders, political participation and so forth. Liu Ji, Vice-President of the Chinese Academy of Social Sciences and an advisor to President Jiang Zemin, argued that without political reform, China will not be able to resolve various major issues. If these issues cannot be resolved, the Party *per se* will be endangered.[26]

4.7 First, corruption has become increasingly serious. In early 1995, Beijing Mayor Chen Xitong's corruption case was exposed. From then on, more and more corruption cases among government officials and Party cadres, especially at the middle and local levels, have also been

---

[26] *Xinbao*, "Liu Ji chengren zhongguo zhengzhi gaige zhihou" ("Liu Ji acknowledged that China's political reform lagged behind"), September 2, 1997.

publicised. Indeed, many top leaders were rather surprised when they found that government positions at local levels could be sold and bought (卖官、买官). If this trend cannot be stopped, the Party as an organisation will break down.[27]

4.8 Furthermore, without a national election system and a free press, it is hard for people to convey their demands and complaints to the leadership. The Party-state has been able to deliver economic benefits to its people due to a growing economic pie. However, rapid development has also resulted in enormous undesirable consequences such as corruption, massive unemployment, money worship, officials' coercive behaviour, worsening public security, ethnic nationalism, workers' strikes and so on. If these various issues cannot be handled properly and promptly, political trouble will follow. Major leaders need to be sensitive about these issues in their decision-making. Even though public opinions cannot be the basis of decision-making, they have to consider public reaction to their policies. Without some forms of interaction between the state and society, political stability will be doubtful. With political stability as its priority, it is understandable that the top leadership cannot afford to democratise China. Therefore, it has to provide people with other means of political participation and at least channels for the public to express their opinions. It also needs to establish mechanisms to constrain government officials' coercive behaviour.

---

[27] On corruption of the CCP, see Yan Huai, "Corruption in China", Part I and II, *IEAPE background Brief* Nos. 73 and 74, 14 October 1994; and IEAPE Correspondent, "Increasing seriousness of corruption in China," *IEAPE background Brief* No. 84, 8 March 1995. On the Chen Xitong case, see, IEAPE Correspondent, "Resignation of Beijing Party Chief Chen Xitong—A politically motivated but limited move against corruption", *IEAPE Commentaries* No. 15, 12 June 1995.

4.9 Third, power succession still matters significantly for the country. China still lacks a mechanism for power succession. Old revolutionaries did not find much difficulty in choosing their own heirs. Deng Xiaoping was able to select or dethrone his own heirs. Without the Old Guards, the Jiang-centred leadership will encounter enormous difficulties over power succession. Apparently, Jiang does not have much choice in selecting his own heir.[28] For the Party, Jiang needs to get something done. Institutionalising the selection process thus became important for the Party to avoid a power succession crisis.

4.10 Therefore, calls for political reform have arisen among some social and political groups.[29] As a response, Jiang and other major leaders began to talk about political reform before the 15th Party Congress. Different from Zhao's time, Jiang and his leadership no longer talked about political reform ideologically. In pre-15th Congress discussions, Chinese intellectuals talked about "implicit political reform" (隐性政治改革). The term means that changes need to be introduced into China's political practice rather than to its political discourse. This is largely reflected in Jiang's political agenda at this congress. From the rhetorical point of view, nothing is new in Jiang's discussion about political reform. But this does not mean that Jiang's attempt on this regard is not important, as many journalists have interpreted.[30] As a matter of fact, what Jiang did is to introduce more institutional elements into China's political system. By doing so, Jiang expects to lay down an institutional foundation for China's further

---

[28] On Jiang's weakness, see Richard Baum, "The jockeying for power", *Asian Wall Street Journal*, September 11, 1997.
[29] Kathy Chen, "Wider range of voices speaks up in China: Louder reform calls resonate ahead of Communist Party Congress," *Asian Wall Street Journal*, September 11, 1997.
[30] For example, according to Jasper Becker, "Despite the growing calls for political reform, President Jiang Zemin outlined only the smallest steps to change the Leninist system", *South China Morning Post*, September 13, 1997.

Power to Set Own Agenda 55

political reform while maintaining political stability. Four aspects merit discussion.

4.11 First of all, the Party leadership proposed to the Congress a draft of the method of electing members of the Central Committee of the CCP. Although there had been various discussions within and outside the Party, the Party never brought up such a proposal for formal discussion. This is important for China's elite recruitment system and power succession. Unlike the Old Guards, the new leaders, without revolutionary experience, do not have a sound base of their political legitimacy. Top leaders can no longer appoint their own heirs at will. Elections will thus become an increasingly important method for selecting Party elites. A working election system without doubt will reinforce the Party leadership's legitimacy among Party members. This move also means that the Party top leadership attempts to develop a mechanism for democracy within the Party (党内民主).

4.12 Second, anti-corruption is another major concern of Jiang's programme of political reform. Even though business is as usual, Jiang's emphasis is on using legal methods to cope with the issues. Jiang stressed the importance of people's supervision on government officials and Party cadres' corruption behaviour. Nevertheless, his central concern is how an effective legal system can be established to constrain corruption. Therefore, as long to be expected, the Party Congress decided to transfer Chen Xitong's case to the court after Chen was punished by Party disciplines.

4.13 Third, Jiang has no intention of expanding Chinese democracy in terms of the relations between the state and society. Nevertheless, he called for consolidating grass-roots democracy. China's rural election system was established in 1987. The system works very impressively considering that the CCP has never had such a democratic experiment before. The top leadership has been very cautious of political participation. Indeed, the implementation of grass-roots democracy has had a positive impact on the CCP. It at least provides a channel for local residents to express their complaints about the Party-state and thus eases the tension between the state and society. As a result, the political legitimacy of the CCP increases. The top leadership has found that the system can be used to elicit "good people" and identify "bad ones". Without doubt, Jiang and his leadership needs such a system to show that the CCP is becoming more democracy-friendly.

4.14 Fourth and more importantly, Jiang Zemin proposed for the first time that the Party would give its highest priority to the rule of law. Since Deng Xiaoping came to power, the CCP has strived to set up an effective legal system. While the rule by law (法制) has been repeatedly emphasised by major Party leaders, the rule of law (法制) is barely mentioned. The rule of law means that the rulers must follow the laws as the ruled do. With increasing crimes committed by Party cadres and government officials, the leadership finds it imperative to use law to constrain and regulate their behaviour. Also, with rising societal demands for political reform, the rule of law seems necessary to mediate and defuse political pressure. While democratisation can lead to chaos, the rule of law can guarantee socio-political stability while it also promotes democracy.

A Party in Transition

5.1 Italian sociologist Vilfredo Pareto argued that power can be quantitatively measured by what one has done.[31] According to Max

---

[31] For an introduction of Pareto's power theory, see Raymond Aron, *Main Currents in Sociological Thought*, vol. 2 (New York: Anchor Books, 1989), Chapter 2.

Weber, when traditional power resources such as ideology and personality are gone, new leaders have to rationalise their power by institution-building.[32]

5.2 This is what Jiang Zemin has done at the Party Congress. Jiang has a good sense of political calculation for himself and for the Party. Having realised that he cannot be a paramount leader like Mao Zedong and Deng Xiaoping, Jiang turns to rely on the Party. As long as he remains the first among equals within the Party leadership, as long as the Party dominates the state and society, Jiang's supreme power position is secured. Certainly, the Party is important for Jiang himself and for the country's development. While Deng Xiaoping transformed the Party from a revolutionary one to an administrative one, Jiang continues to re-build it by introducing various institutional elements. What Jiang has expected is that the Party has to adjust itself to changing socio-economic situations while promoting the country's further development. From the perspective of Party transformation, Jiang has been quite successful.

5.3 First of all, after Deng, Jiang has made the Party's ideology more flexible by re-interpreting the theory of primary stage of socialism. What exactly the theory means is still unclear. What is clear is that the theory is compatible with almost everything, positive and negative. As a popular Chinese adage indicates, "the theory of primary stage is like a basket, you can put in whatever you want" (初级阶理论象个框, 什么东西都可往里装). By re-interpreting the theory, Jiang has showed that the Party's priority is still to develop the country's economy. On the other hand, Jiang has also contended that the various

---

[32] See Max Weber, *The Theory of Social and Economic Organisations*, ed. Talcott Parsons (New York: Free Press, 1964).

"negative" consequences resulting from rapid economic development are temporary and transitional. While the Leftists attribute these undesirable consequences to the reform, Jiang argues that these are the necessary costs of the reform. More importantly, a flexible ideology benefits the Party by making the Party flexible and sensitive to changing socio-economic conditions. As long as the Party can adjust itself to new developments, it will stand as the leading force of Chinese society.

5.4 Second, ideology *per se* does not matter. It needs believers who are willing to understand and behave in accordance with its gist or in Chinese, 精髓. The leadership's commitment to economic priority, however, does matter. Since good economic performance has become the base of the Party's political legitimacy, Jiang needs to recruit dedicated leaders into the Party leadership. Even though the Party top leadership is largely unchanged, more new figures are recruited into other important Party position. As discussed above, new recruits consolidate Jiang's power position. But the Party is strengthened too. With a new generation of leaders coming to the Chinese political hierarchy at different levels, the Party is prepared to lead the country into the 21st century.

5.5 Finally, when the Party's priority is on stability and development, not much can be done about political reform and democracy. After being in power for many years and having witnessed political chaos in Russia, Jiang knows how important the transformation of the Party is. Without a strong Party-state leading political reform or democratisation, chaos will follow. Jiang has a sound rationale to give his priority to the institutional building of the Party-state and the rule of law rather than broader political participation or democracy. With the institutionalisation of the Party-state at the top and the grass-roots democracy taking place below, China's political transformation could be more stable and easier in the next century.

5.6 Nevertheless, Jiang Zemin is not without challenges in implementing his new agenda. Most measures proposed by Jiang like reforming SOEs and curbing corruption are merely "fire-fighting" ones, aiming to cope with the most pressing problems. More importantly, China still lacks an effective legal system. As long as the Leninist Party-state stays above the law, no law will be able to govern the Party *per se*. The rule of law will be impossible. Without Party cadres and government officials' obeying the law, the Party will not be able to restrict their corrupt behaviour, and to strengthen its power. Chinese people probably will have to wait for the fourth, or even fifth generation leaders to bring about full democratisation.

REFORMING CHINA'S STATE-OWNED ENTERPRISES: PROBLEMS AND PROSPECTS

John WONG and SIM Poh Kheng

EXECUTIVE SUMMARY

1. Reform of state-owned enterprises (SOEs) was catapulted to the top economic agenda in the recently concluded 15th Party Congress.
2. The problems of Chinese SOEs, particularly their mounting losses and increasing indebtedness, are indeed well known. But past government efforts of SOE reform (based on the gradual improvement of enterprise governance) have produced no significant results partly because the Chinese leadership did not have the required political will to carry the reform through.
3. Now, with a confident and secure political leadership together with strong economic fundamentals, China is ready to renew its reform efforts in order to crack this daunting problem.
4. China has yet to publish the details of its new reform blueprint. But there are precious few surprises (like the principle of "diverse public ownership" for legitimizing "partial" privatisation) in Jiang's new SOE reform package, presented at this Party Congress. Virtually, all the major proposed measures have either been tried out before or are already in practice. What is really new is the express political determination on the part of the leadership to confront the SOE problem head-on.
5. In terms of implementation, the strategy of *Zhuada fangxiao* (抓大放小) is still the guide. For the large and medium SOEs, the emphasis will still be on improving enterprise governance, i.e. transform them into independent modern corporations with modern management. The Chinese Government will help them to corporatise with financial assistance.

6. For the numerous smaller SOEs controlled by provincial and municipal governments, they will be given more options to revitalise themselves, through restructuring and reorganisation, mergers and take-overs, leasing and management contract, conversion into shareholding companies, or even sell-off. More shake-ups and more laid-offs will be expected from these smaller SOEs.
7. Zhu Rongji confidently said that the SOE problem could be sorted out in about three years. He may have sounded a little too optimistic, for a lot of SOE problems defy simple technocratic solutions.
8. The reformed SOEs certainly need time to adjust to modern management culture, and they have to learn to behave as competitive business units. But it now looks possible for China to "fix" its SOE problem, not in a matter of a few years, but more likely in 10 years.

REFORMING CHINA'S STATE-OWNED ENTERPRISES: PROBLEMS AND PROSPECTS

John WONG and SIM Poh Kheng[#]

Coming to Grips with the SOE Problem

1.1 One of the most intractable problems for all reforming transitional economies is how to cope with their ailing state-owned enterprises (SOEs). Chinese reformers, despite their eminent success in their overall economic reform efforts, have been similarly dogged by the same problem. In late 1993, China introduced a comprehensive economic reform programme to bring about a "socialist market economy", and it has generally achieved impressive results (e.g. reform of the tax and foreign exchange systems) except in the critical area of SOE reform, which has yet to experience important breakthrough.[1] Why has the SOE problem still eluded Chinese reformers? Lacking a favourable macroeconomic environment apart, fundamentally the Chinese leadership did not have the required political will to face up to the problems of the SOE reform.

[#] Professor John Wong is Research Director of the East Asian Institute. Miss Sim Poh Kheng is Research Officer of the Institute.
[1] For further discussion of China's past economic reform progress, see John Wong, "What has China accomplished in economic reform in 1994?", *IEAPE Background Brief* No. 80 (December 13, 1994).

1.2 In the recently concluded 15th National Party Congress (12–18 September 1997), however, reform of SOEs was catapulted to the top of the economic agenda. The political and economic significance of this decisive move is obvious. Politically, Jiang Zemin must have now felt sufficiently secure as to dare to tackle the daunting SOE problem.[2] Economically, the Chinese leadership has long realized that a bold, comprehensive attack on the SOE problem is needed in order to complete the unfinished business of economic reform. Without sorting out its SOE problem, China cannot proceed to accomplish its much-needed financial sector reform. As long as these two critical areas remain in limbo, China will not complete its transition to a full market system and will continue to suffer from the inefficiency of a partially reformed economy. Now with the Chinese economy continuing its high growth and low inflation, this would indeed be strategically the best time for China to come to grips with the SOE problem.[3]

1.3 SOE reform is an enormously difficult undertaking as it goes beyond simple economics and involves many larger political and social issues. In fully committing itself to this difficult task, the technocratically-inclined Jiang leadership has clearly calculated the possible political and economic risks. As warned by a recent World Bank report, any mishandling of the SOE problem by the Chinese government could engender social instability in the urban areas and

---

[2] Many China experts have been quite surprised by the ways in which Jiang had maneuvered the other potential power contender, Qiao Shi, out of the Standing Committee of China's Politburo at the 15th Party Congress. For a more detailed analysis of the post-Party Congress politics in China, see Zheng Yongnian and Zou Ziying, "Power to set own agenda: Jiang Zemin's new political initiative at China's 15th Party Congress", *EAI Background Brief* No. 2 (September 26, 1997).

[3] For a succinct analysis of the present state of China's economy, see John Wong, "Good political arithmetick: China's economy on the eve of the Fifteenth Party Congress", *EAI Background Brief* No. 1 (September 2, 1997).

slow down China's economic growth. But the present top leadership seems quite upbeat about their ability to cope with the SOE reform problem, as they believe they have already had a good grasp of the whole situation. In fact, at the recent IMF/World Bank meeting in Hong Kong, Zhu Rongji confidently said that China could sort out the loss making problem of its SOEs in about three years.

1.4 Will China succeed in reforming its problematic SOEs in a matter of few years? The SOE issue, despite extensive media coverage and debates during the 15th Party Congress, is still surrounded by a great deal of public misconception. There is indeed considerable confusion, both inside and outside China, over the true state of affairs of China's SOEs in terms of their numbers, their actual conduct and performance, their linkages to the other sectors of the Chinese economy and so on. This paper seeks to clarify China's SOE reform efforts and the related problems.

The Cumbersome State Sector

2.1 SOEs or *guoyou qiye* (国有企业) are essentially products of socialism. In China, SOEs used to function primarily as socio-economic entities rather than as purely production units. The objective function of many large SOEs is not limited to maximizing profits. Their operations include the provision of such social and welfare services, normally considered "public goods" such as education, medical services, housing, child care services and pensions.[4] Indeed, many large SOEs exist much like "mini-welfare states"; and not surprisingly,

---

[4] The Anshan Steel used to be the case where only about one third of those on its payroll were the "production people" directly linked to steel making, about one-third were service workers and the other one-third were pensioners.

they operate under "soft budget constraints", with the government always ready to subsidize their losses.

2.2 Chinese and foreign media have added to the public confusion by using different sets of figures for the total number of SOEs and their different sizes. Latest official statistics from the *China Statistical Yearbook 1996* shows that China has about 320,000 SOEs, out of which some 240,000 are commonly classified as "small".[5] Of the 320,000 SOEs, only some 118,000 are engaged in industrial production, and about 16,000 are classified "large and medium".[6] There is considerable ambiguity as to how SOEs are exactly classified according to size, and how they are considered as "industrial" and "non-industrial". Conceptually, all SOEs are supposed to come under the state's control; but it is not clear how many SOEs actually report to the central government, and how many are under the direct administrative control of the local governments of provinces, cities and counties. Further, there is even less published information regarding the SOEs run by the PLA (People's Liberation Army) and those controlled by the Commission of Science, Technology and Industry for National Defence as defence industry.

2.3 In 1978, SOEs accounted for 78% of China's total industrial output. By 1996 (as shown in Table 1), the share declined to 29%. But the lower output share of the state sector should not be misconstrued as its diminishing economic importance, since 108.5 million or 74% of the urban working population (*Zhi-gong* (职工) or "staff and workers") currently still rely on the SOEs to provide them with some

---

[5] See Premier Li Peng's "Government Work Report" presented at the National People's Congress in March 1997 (*Zhongguo gongshang shibao*, 2 March 1997).
[6] *China Statistical Yearbook, 1996*.

Table 1. Gross Industrial Output in China, 1978–1996.

(RMB billion)

Year	Total industrial output	State-owned enterprises		Non state-owned enterprises				
				Sector as a whole		Of which: collective-owned enterprises		
		Output	% Share*	Output^A	% Share*	Output^B	% Share*
1978	423.7	328.9	77.6	94.8	22.4	94.8	22.4
1980	515.4	391.6	76.0	123.8	24.0	121.3	23.5
1985	971.6	630.2	64.9	341.4	35.1	311.7	32.1
1986	1119.4	697.1	62.3	422.3	37.7	375.2	33.5
1987	1381.3	825.0	59.7	556.3	40.3	478.2	34.6
1988	1822.4	1035.1	56.8	787.3	43.2	658.8	36.2
1989	2201.7	1234.3	56.1	967.4	43.9	785.8	35.7
1990	2392.4	1306.4	54.6	1086.0	45.4	852.3	35.6
1991	2662.5	1495.5	56.2	1167.0	43.8	878.3	33.0
1992	3459.9	1782.4	51.5	1677.5	48.5	1213.5	35.1
1993	4840.2	2272.5	47.0	2567.7	53.0	1646.4	34.0
1994	7017.6	2620.1	37.3	4397.5	62.7	2647.2	37.7
1995	8229.7	2684.1	32.6	5545.6	67.4	2925.3	35.5
1996	9949.3	2868.3	28.8	7081.0	71.2	4016.7	40.4

Note: * denotes "as a percentage share of total industrial output".
Source: *The Statistical Survey of China 1997* (Beijing).

form of "cradle-to-grave" employment.[7] Furthermore, the state sector as a whole still controls approximately 61% of the total state assets and constitutes some 55% of total domestic sales. In terms of foreign trade, about 67% of China's exports and 50% of imports in 1995 were conducted through the foreign trading arm of the state firms. From the standpoint of the government, the economic importance of the state sector in the Chinese economy is reflected in its traditional role as a major source of central government tax revenue (Table 2). Chart 1 shows that the non-state sector contributes less than half to total government revenue.

2.4   Viewed from a different angle, the relative decline of the SOE sector since the reform merely reflects the dynamic expansion of the non-state sector, particularly the township and village enterprises (TVEs) and various forms of individual enterprises and foreign ventures. In fact, SOEs are still predominant in key areas of heavy industry such as iron and steel, coal, metallurgy, chemicals, energy production, and petroleum exploration, which have to operate on the economies of scale and are generally shunned by the TVEs or denied to foreign investors. Also, some 80% of China's basic industrial raw materials and a wide range of intermediate products have continued to be produced by SOEs.

2.5   In recent years, China has started to publish its own "Fortune 500", most of which are essentially SOEs, including the annual best performing "Top Three".[8] So are those "Red Chips" enterprises, which

---

[7] This employment figure refers to the end of June 1997 (China Economic Information Service of the Xinhua News Agency, August 6, 1997). China's employment statistics is confusing and can be misleading because of its peculiar definition of "unemployment" and complicated classification of "urban" and "rural" employment.

[8] For instance, in 1994, the "Top Three", in terms of profits and taxes, are the three largest iron and steel corporation of Baoshan, Shougang and Anshan ("State firms still

Table 2. Profits & Taxes of State Enterprises (1978–1994).

(RMB billion)

Year	Total government tax revenue (A)	SOE total profits & taxes		Ratio of C/A (%)
		Profits (B)	Taxes (C)	
1978	51.93	73.35	33.13	63.8
1980	57.17	66.92	38.24	66.9
1981	62.99	64.31	40.77	64.7
1982	70.00	63.15	43.88	62.7
1983	77.56	69.65	45.55	58.7
1984	94.74	78.89	51.47	54.3
1985	204.08	99.88	69.49	34.1
1986	209.07	79.51	74.52	35.6
1987	214.04	98.15	86.51	40.4
1988	239.05	116.49	105.06	43.9
1989	272.74	100.12	123.23	45.2
1990	282.19	49.15	123.10	43.6
1991	299.02	74.45	139.29	46.6
1992	329.69	95.52	155.54	47.2
1993	425.53	166.73	197.58	46.4
1994	512.69	160.80	223.63	43.6

Sources:
1. *The Statistical Survey of China 1996* (Beijing).
2. *China Statistical Yearbook 1996* (Beijing).

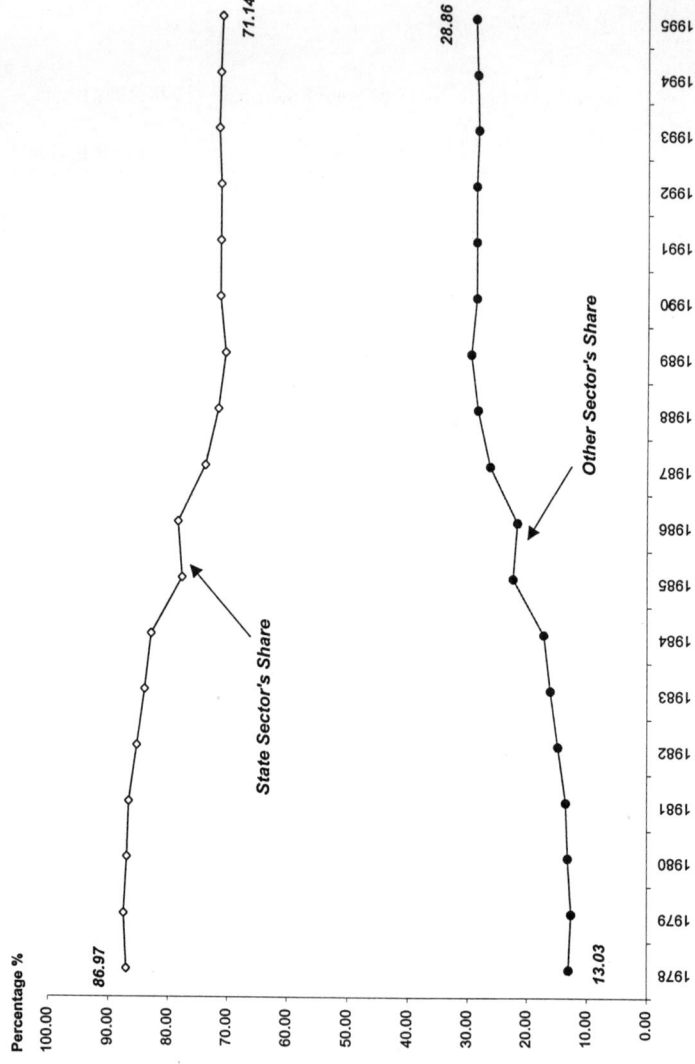

Chart 1: CONTRIBUTION TO GOVERNMENT REVENUE (1978 - 1995) IN PERCENTAGE TERMS

Source: *China Statistical Yearbook 1996*

have already been listed as "H shares" on the Hong Kong Stock Exchange and the "N shares" on the New York Stock Exchange. But this picture of China having many "good SOEs" can be misleading. In 1993, the Chinese government announced that about one third of its SOEs were reported to have made losses, with another one-third just breaking even. The proportion of loss-making SOEs has since been increasing and by the first half of 1997, 47% of all SOEs were reporting losses.

2.6 It may be rather meaningless to speak of real "profit and losses" of any enterprise operating in China's present half-reformed economy without credible and transparent public accounting and auditing systems. Many SOEs still do not function like profit-maximizing firms in market-oriented economy. Some make profits because of their monopoly position in a particular sector. Others have to incur losses for non-economic reasons (e.g. to carry out their socio-political mandate) or because of price controls (e.g. coal, gas, fertilizer and essential commodity items during the anti-inflationary period). Premier Li Peng, during his recent visit to Singapore in August 1997, pointed out that the extent of China's SOEs losses had been grossly exaggerated by foreign media. And Mr. Li may be right.

2.7 Regardless of the real extent of the SOE losses and their real causes, it is widely acknowledged that the overall performance of China's SOEs has remained weak. Suffice to say that China's inefficient

play major role in economy", *China Daily*, August 25,1994). In 1995, the Daqing Petroleum ranked first. (Xinhua News Agency, English Service, April 11, 1995). China also compiled its top 500 Import and Export Firms in terms of turnover, and virtually most of them are SOEs because until recent years the state had a monopoly in foreign trade. In 1996, all the top ten are the former national trading corporations (*China Economic News*, No. 6, August 11, 1997, Supplement).

SOE sector poses three major economic problems: (1) A beleaguered SOE sector controlling a disproportionately large share of physical and human resources represents a clear case of massive misallocation of resources in the economy; (2) The continuing subsidy to cover SOE losses by the government has been a significant cause of China's chronic fiscal deficits; and (3) an unreformed SOE sector presents a major hindrance to the financial sector reform as state banks, under obligation to bail out ailing SOEs, have incurred colossal amounts of bad debts and non-performing loans, estimated to be around 25%.[9]

Tardy Progress in SOE Reform

3.1 It is common knowledge that one fundamental economic solution to the SOE problem is to subject SOEs to real "hard budget constraints"—i.e. closing down those which are financially not viable. In this regard, efforts must be made to de-couple the production function of SOEs from their non-production social obligations, which ultimately entails breaking the traditional "three *irons*" guarantee—iron rice bowl, iron position and iron wages. But politically and socially, this would not be a viable option for China until a new social safety net is well in place. Otherwise, it would run the risk of throwing tens of millions of workers into the streets. This could possibly explain why China's bankruptcy law, first introduced in 1986, had seldom been used as a mean to attack the SOE problem.

---

[9] A Monetary Authority of Singapore (MAS) team recently made a fact-finding study trip to China to understand the policy direction of SOE reforms and the contribution of the financial system to the latter. The study found that the proportion of SOEs making losses rose from 26 percent in 1992 to 44 percent to 1995, with debt-assets ratios as high as 85 percent ("Recent Developments in China's State-owned Enterprise Reform and Financial Reform: Study Trip Report, 28–31 July 1997", External Economic Division, Monetary Authority of Singapore).

3.2 The other fundamental solution is to go for a wholesale privatization as it has been done in the former Soviet Union and other East European socialist states. But again, this would not be a viable option for China as the Chinese Communist Party has remained, until this day, ideologically opposed to the idea of open privatization. In any case, such a "Big Bang" approach to economic reform (adopted by the East European socialists with dismal results) has never been the hallmark of China's style of economic reform, which is characterized by its cautious and gradualist approach based on "learning by doing".

3.3 Prior to 1993, the reform of SOEs in China was based mainly on improving enterprise governance with emphasis on progressive increase in managerial autonomy and accountability. Reform efforts in the early 1980s first started with the "profit retention scheme" (*lirun liucheng*) and the "contract responsibility system" (*zifu yinkui*); and subsequently, the introduction of "tax for profit system" (*li-gai-shui*). At the same time, urban price reform was slowly introduced along with measures taken to decentralize planning and increase reliance on market forces for price management, commodity and factor markets, investment financing, foreign trade, and foreign exchange. The idea was to reduce the overall level of price distortion in the economy, which in turn would bring about a more conducive external macroeconomic environment for SOEs to operate closer to market conditions. Open privatization was, of course, not actively promoted as it would run into ideological conflict with the Party's orthodoxy; but "covert privatization" in the form of "shareholding companies" was quietly experimented, mainly by local-level SOEs.

3.4 Moving so gingerly, all these reform efforts had naturally achieved no substantive results. By the early 1990s, the basic socialistic *modus operandi* of China's SOEs, particularly for the large ones, remained unchanged. But new economic crises began to envelop the SOE sector. As a result of the government's post-Tiananmen credit crunch, many SOEs came into grief after having made heavy losses. Many more were trapped in a serious "Triangular Debt" involving both enterprises and state banks.[10] Apart from being a serious threat to the financial sector, these debt-ridden SOEs also imposed high fiscal burden on the government, which is obliged to subsidize their losses.[11] The Chinese leadership, therefore, had no choice but to renew its efforts to cope with the SOE problem.

3.5 Following Deng Xiaoping's tour of South China in 1992, China unleashed a new reform momentum in order to realize the so-called "socialist market economy". In the amended Constitution approved by the 8th National People's Congress in March 1993, the name "state enterprise" or *guoying qiye* (literally, "state-run enterprise (国营企业)") was formally changed to *guoyou qiye* (literally, "state-owned enterprise (国有企业)"). This simple change in name was sufficiently significant as it sets out to make a distinction between enterprise ownership and enterprise management, a clear implication that the government is no

---

[10] "Triangular Debt" refers to a situation whereby Firm A owes Firm B, Firm B owes Firm C, Firm C owes Firm D, and the chain runs on. The government has sought to end this vicious cycle by injecting large funds into the system but as soon as the old debt chain is eliminated, new ones start to appear. The "Triangular Debts" could possibly be stopped if a "hard budget constraint" were imposed on the SOEs, allowing the inefficient ones to go bust. But this is politically impossible and socially disastrous in the absence of a social security net and welfare system to grapple with unemployment pressures.

[11] When SOEs make losses, the government has to subsidize their losses directly in the form of budget transfers, which amounted to 1.4% of GDP in 1994. But for those which have manage to break even, the government still has to provide them with implicit financial subsidies in the form of cheap loans and lax repayment, and this amounted to an additional 1.7% of GDP in 1994. Total subsidies were even higher before, e.g. 8% in 1987. See World Bank, *China: Reform of State-Owned Enterprises* (June 21, 1996).

longer under obligation to be administratively involved in direct enterprise management. SOEs are officially owned by the state but technically, they are to be managed by themselves, as in the case of Singapore's government-linked companies. In other words, SOEs can now incorporate various market-oriented systems.

3.6 During the period of 1993–97, the main thrust of the SOE reform efforts has been directed towards the establishment of a "modern enterprise system", which was also incorporated into the comprehensive economic reform package adopted by the Third Party Plenum in November 1993. Specifically, apart from promoting further improvement in enterprise governance through "scientific" (modern) management, the government placed major emphasis on corporatization. Thus, SOEs were encouraged to develop into a profitable "modern enterprise system" by restructuring their internal operations and incentive structures, or to form into new enterprise groups or *qiye jituan* (企业集团) through mergers and acquisitions or other forms of integration. In the meanwhile, the experimentation of the shareholding system was also stepped up. In fact, Chinese reformers even looked into the Japanese *keiretsu* and South Korean *chaebols* for lessons of experience. Above all, the Company Law was enacted in July 1994 in order to provide a modern legal framework for the corporatization drive.

3.7 In early 1995, China's SOE reform efforts crystallized further into a more explicit strategy of *Zhuada Fangxiao* (抓大放小) or "nurturing the big [into giant conglomerates] while letting go the small SOEs [to the forces of market mechanism]". The government has apparently taken the view that while they could "let go" the 240,000 or so small, mainly local-level SOEs, via various forms of restructuring including reorganization, mergers and takeover, leasing and management contract, conversion into shareholding companies, or even outright closure, they must and will retain the 1,000 large SOEs belonging to the central government, for obvious economic and social reasons. These key SOEs are still of strategic importance as they constitute the backbone of China's industrial economy in terms of total capitalization and employment. As mentioned earlier, some of these SOEs are not doing so badly. Socially, they are just too important to be allowed to go bust, for fear of widespread urban unemployment.

3.8 In his "Government Work Report" presented to the National People Congress in March 1997, Premier Li Peng confirmed that in 1996, of the 1,000 targeted SOEs, 300 of them had improved their performance after the injection of fresh state bank loans along with tighter financial control, and an additional 57 SOEs had formed into modern enterprise groups.[12] Year after year, the Chinese government has continued to provide huge financial resources to large SOEs just to ensure their survival and in the hope that they would eventually perform. What have been the results?

3.9 On the whole, the decade-long government efforts of grappling with the SOE reform problem have obviously produced no significant breakthrough. This is plainly evident from repeated official acknowledgment of mounting SOE losses and continuing indebtedness of SOEs. A recent survey conducted on 124,000 state enterprises showed the asset-liability ratio of SOEs lying within the range of 71.5% to 83.3%.[13] Reasons for the persistent poor

---

[12] "The 6-Measure of Promoting SOE Reform", *Zhongguo Gongshang Shibao* (China Industrial and Commercial Times, Beijing, March 2, 1997).
[13] "Workers Daily says that State-Owned Firms are Bottomless Pits", *South China Morning Post*, August 30, 1997.

performance of SOEs are also plain enough. Basically many large SOEs are still not operating entirely under "hard budget constraints". This is partly due to the sluggish progress in the social security reform. But many SOEs have yet to develop a modern, market-oriented management culture. Their management knows only too well that state banks are always on hand to bail them out if they run into financial distress. At the local levels, the SOE reform suffered from a host of malpractice and corruption like "fraudulent bankruptcy (假破产)"[14] and the "three disorderliness (三乱)"—disorderly fee collection, disorderly levies and disorderly fund raising.

3.10 It may be stressed that China's top economic priority in the past few years was to cool its overheating economy. Therefore, the government did not really push ahead vigorously with its SOE reform agenda. Indeed, the various austerity measures introduced by Zhu Rongji since late 1993 for macroeconomic stabilization tended to "squeeze" many SOEs and actually aggravated their woes. Such continuing deterioration of the SOE financial conditions has, in retrospect, made both the government and the industry realize the urgent need for a more thorough-going reform of the SOE sector. Thus, on the eve of the 15th Party Congress, the problem of SOE reform weighed heavily upon the Chinese leadership.

New Measures for Old Problems?

4.1 The timing for the decisive move on the SOE reform by the Chinese leadership was just right: (1) Politically, much to the surprise

---

[14] Some firms have hidden agendas to rid themselves of debt and interest burdens by declaring themselves bankrupt, even though their financial situations might not render such a drastic measure. State banks, on the other hand, were generally reluctant in

of many observers, Jiang Zemin has emerged as an unchallenged leader in the post-Deng power struggle. A secure and undivided top leadership is crucial for making hard reform decisions. (2) China's economy, having achieved a successful "soft landing" is apparently heading for a new era of sustainable high growth with low inflation. Strong economic growth will generate more resources for the authorities to cope with the troubled SOEs. Specifically in the context of China, this also means that the non-state sector will continue to expand, thereby cushioning the adverse impact of the SOE reform. (3) Apart from a confident political leadership and strong economic fundamentals, Chinese reformers have by now more or less grasped the full technicality of their SOE reform problem, thanks to the bold experimentation on a wide front over the past few years.

4.2 Indeed, Jiang has been preparing the political and ideological ground for the new SOE reform strategy well ahead of the 15th Party Congress. As noted earlier, it has been an ideological taboo in China to openly advocate "private ownership", which would immediately evoke strong reaction from the conservative Party ideologues and spark off the old debate on the relative virtues of socialism and capitalism—the so-called "Mr. Socialist (姓社) vs. Mr. Capitalist (姓资)" argument. This explains why the past SOE reform strategy had deliberately avoided a direct attack on the "state ownership" issue by playing down the "privatization" aspects of the reform, so as not to cross such ideological off-limits. Jiang had to soften such ideological opposition beforehand. What Jiang did, in simple terms, was essentially to urge Chinese people to put aside futile debates over

---

pushing for more bankruptcies as this would mean writing off huge debts from their balance sheets. In 1996, out of the total number of bankruptcy cases accredited, less than 2 percent (72 cases out of 6232) were initiated by banks (*Jingji Cankaobao*, Beijing , January 28, 1997).

the "public vs. private ownership" by calling for "the third liberalization of thought",[15] and to remind his leftist critic that China is presently still in the transitional "primary stage of socialism", which would therefore warrant having "diverse forms of ownership to develop side by side" and "diverse economic sectors to develop side by side".[16] This implied flexibility in changing the ownership structure of SOEs, thus filling an important gap in the previous reform efforts, which encountered difficulty in coping with SOEs' weak internal incentive mechanism associated with ownership and controls.

4.3 Jiang's proposed reform package presented at the 15th Party Congress is based on a multi-pronged approach. What is really new? China has not yet published the detailed SOE reform blueprint, which will probably be revealed at the next National People's Congress in early 1998. But judging from Jiang's Party Congress speech, there is actually not much that is new in terms of policy initiative, except for the principle of "diversification of public ownership", (which would facilitate SOEs to privatize parts of their operations and assets). In

---

[15] In the weeks of run-up to the Party Congress, the Party's Propaganda Department had urged cadres to seriously study Jiang's speech on the "third liberalization of thought, based on seeking truth from facts", delivered at the Central Party School in May 1997. The "first liberalization" was advocated by Deng Xiaoping in 1978 calling for a more flexible interpretation of Mao's thoughts in order to prepare China for economic reform and the open-door policy. The second liberalization" was again advocated by Deng in 1992 during his "tour of South China", urging people to put behind the futile debate over "Socialism vs. Capitalism" so that China could move into a "socialist market economy". This time, Jiang , in calling for the "third liberalization", was asking the Chinese people to forget about the debate on "public vs. private ownership", so that he can go ahead with his SOE reform plans (*Xinbao, Hong Kong Economic Journal*, August 15, 1997).

[16] Jiang Zemin's Report to the 15th Party Congress on September 12, 1997 entitled "Hold high the great banner of Deng Xiaoping theory for an all-round advancement of the cause of building socialism with Chinese characteristics to the 21st century".

terms of actual implementation, the basic strategy will be much like the *Zhuada Fangxiao* (抓大放小).

4.4 For the large and medium SOEs, the reform will still be on improving enterprise governance but the emphasis is on "corporatization" or transforming SOEs into independent modern corporations based on "scientific" (modern) management. In this regard, more than 500 SOEs have already been earmarked for corporatization and another 120 SOEs to form into enterprise groups by 1997. Rmb 30 billion has been set aside to recapitalize these firms. Thus, some will merge, some will break up, some will seek foreign partnership, and some will seek listing on the stock exchanges in Shanghai, Shenzhen, Hong Kong and possibly, Singapore.

4.5 For the numerous smaller SOEs, the main reform strategy remains pretty much the same. But the government will now be much more willing to "let go", virtually allowing them to pick whichever ways that will best revitalize themselves—through restructuring and reorganization, mergers and takeovers, leasing and management contract, conversion into shareholding companies or even sell-off. Since private ownership is no longer such an ideological minefield, certainly more SOEs will be converted into shareholding companies this time. It will also be easier for firms to declare bankruptcy and be sold out, even to foreign partners.

4.6 These smaller SOEs will be given more options and greater flexibility to choose their reform paths. Many of them are already engaging in potentially competitive activities that do not really need the presence of the state. The "dynamics" of the reform is more likely to be felt at the provincial and municipal SOEs than at the large ones controlled by the central government. At the same time, unlike those larger SOEs earmarked for priority government assistance in finance and technological upgrading, reform of smaller SOEs will obviously experience more shake-ups, hence more laid-offs and retrenchment of workers, either openly or disguised in the name of *Xia-gang* (下岗). Jiang has already warned about such inevitability.

4.7 In the pre-Congress debate on the SOE reform, a lot of discussion had been focused on the shareholding system (particularly the "shareholding cooperatives"), which technically speaking is the Chinese form of "privatization in disguise". The shareholding scheme can address the crucial state ownership issue more effectively—i.e. without owning a stake in the enterprise, its workers and management do not have the inherent incentive to perform well. However, in Jiang's speech, the shareholding system was not singled out for special attention, probably because the authorities have yet to sort out the technicalities associated with large-scale promotion of the shareholding system, especially the "shareholding cooperatives".[17]

4.8 In summary, there are precious few surprises in Jiang's new SOE reform package as presented at the recent 15th Party Congress. Virtually, all the major proposed measures have either been tried out before or are already in practice. What is really new is the express

---

[17] Many standard technical issues remain to be dealt with, e.g. how a shareholding company values its assets and how it will divide up the shares for allotment among the state or local government, the enterprise's own employees, and such legal entities as banks, pension funds etc. Currently, the controversial issue is on whether or not each worker is allowed to vote as one shareholder regardless of the number of shares he holds, and how he can buy and sell his shares on the secondary market. Particularly for the "shareholding cooperative", some legal scholars have argued that it is "neither a horse nor a mule", as it displays a contradictory mixture of the capitalist element of shareholding along with the socialist element of a cooperative.

political will on the part of China's top leadership along with declining social resistance to confront the SOE problem head-on, which was conspicuously absent in the previous reform efforts.

Jiang Might Just Pull it Off

5.1 Jiang has adroitly used Deng's reform achievements ("Holding high the great banner of Deng Xiaoping Theory (高举邓小平理论伟大旗帜)") to legitimize his new reform initiatives and to allay possible public anxiety over future reform risks. Deng has been called the "architect of China's economic reform" for having initiated the reform process. Now Jiang is left to complete the rest, which is politically and technically more difficult to manage.

5.2 Jiang has to carefully calculate the ensuing risks and costs. The *Xia-gang* (下岗) problem is now getting more serious in the urban areas. Will Jiang still push ahead with more drastic restructuring and retrenchment of SOEs in the absence of an adequate social security system and a viable retraining programme?[18] According to China's Labour Ministry, 3.7 million workers will lose their jobs this year as a result of SOE reform, alongside with the annual new entrants to the

---

See, "Shareholding cooperatives are in urgent need of proper legal rulings", *Xinbao* (*Hong Kong Economic Journal*) August 30, 1997.

[18] The "*Xia Gang* (下岗)" phenomenon is in itself an innovative way by the Chinese government to grapple with unemployment pressures. Despite suffering from many flaws, laid-off SOE employees are still ensured a minimal level retrenchment benefits by their former employer until they are re-deployed. As the SOE reform gains momentum, it is plausible to anticipate the emergence of a shrinking state sector, with concomitant expansion of the non-state sector and a robust tertiary industry. While the state concentrates on a few selected industry giants, the non-state sector (consisting of collectives, individuals and those with foreign investment) will gain importance in terms of its contribution to China's economic growth and job creation. Some cities

labour force of 14 million.[19] The total number of redundant workers in SOEs as estimated by the World Bank is about 15 million, which can be a potentially explosive problem in terms of visible urban unemployment and the related high social security burdens.[20] Hence, the great challenge for Jiang.

5.3 Jiang is fortunate to have Deng's well-tried reform strategy as his guide. By avoiding the bureaucratic approach by issuing a highly structured reform programme with declared targets to fulfill, Jiang's reform strategy is actually in line with the old practice of "crossing the river by touching the stone (摸着石头过河)". In other words, if the reform should run into strong resistance in some sectors or some cities, the reform process would simply slow down to avail itself of the next opportunity—"Taking two steps forward and (if in trouble) one step back".

5.4 It is also in the nature of the Chinese past reform practice for the central government to provide only a clear mandate with broad guidelines. This will then be picked up by local authorities to start

such as Shanghai, Chongqing and municipals of Guangdong province have been quite successful in solving the problem of surplus workers. It is probably less problematic for regions with high foreign investment and a flourishing service sector which are channels of reemployment opportunities. In the case of Shanghai, its current unemployment rate is controlled within 2 to 3 percent, with some 150,000 to 200,000 officially classified as "unemployed". In 1996, some 230,000 workers were made redundant but all of them have been re-employed. In Chongqing, some 30 percent of its retrenched SOE employees have been absorbed into the private sector in the last two years ("Promising Re-employment Project", *Beijing Review*, August 1997).

[19] Dentusche Presse-Agentur, September 22 1997 (Dow Jones News/Retrieval).
[20] One source puts the total number of laid-off workers resulting from SOE reform as 8 million in the next five years, and their unemployment benefits will cost the state Rmb 160 billion.
See "Big talk, little progress", *China Trade Report* (April 1996).

reforming on their own initiative and in accordance with their own conditions. In this way, local governments will create their own reform momentum. It can be expected the more capitalist-inclined coastal cities and coastal provinces will quickly seize the favourable reform climate and start their own innovative solution to the SOE problem.

5.5 In hoping to "sort things out" in about three years, Zhu Rongji does sound a little too optimistic. He probably reckons that with the Chinese economy expected to grow at an annual average rate of 8% up to 2010, the economic costs of the SOE reform could be easily absorbed. What is needed for his reform efforts is continuing political and social consensus, which is steadily taking root. China might just be able to "fix" its SOE problem, not in a matter of a few years, but more likely in 10 years.

5.6 Given the current dominance of the state sector, in terms of physical, financial and human resources, and its social responsibilities and contribution to government revenue, it would have to take a longer time for the reform process to reap visible and real benefits for both the firms and the economy. China's SOEs are plagued not merely by "hard problems" such as capital shortage and outdated technology and equipment, but also by a host of equally serious "soft problems" such as corruption, nepotism, and socialistic style of management and work habit, which defy simple technocratic solutions. China certainly needs many years to put in place a functioning legal framework. It also takes time for the reformed SOEs to learn to behave as competitive business units.

LIST OF CONTRIBUTORS

John WONG
Professor Wong is Research Director of the East Asian Institute, Singapore. He was formerly Director of the Institute of East Asian Political Economy (IEAPE). His previous publications include *ASEAN Economies in Perspective, Understanding China's Socialist Market Economy* and *Land Reform in the People's Republic of China*, as well as numerous papers on the economic development of China, ASEAN and Asian NIEs.

ZHENG Yongnian
Dr. Zheng obtained his Ph.D in Politics from Princeton University in 1995. Currently a Research Fellow of East Asian Institute, he was formerly a research fellow in Harvard University's SSRC-MacArthur Foundation of International Peace and Security. Dr. Zheng has published in various journals such as *Political Science Quarterly, Asian Survey, Pacific Review and Asian Affairs*. He recently finished a book manuscript entitled *Discovering Chinese Nationalism in China: Modernization and International Relations*.

ZOU Ziying
Mr. Zou graduated from Beijing University, majoring in Economics. An erudite scholar in China's political and economic development, he has previously served in various important government organs and ministries in China. Mr. Zou, who joined the former Institute of East Asian Political Economy (IEAPE) in 1995, is currently a Research Fellow of the East Asian Institute.

SIM Poh Kheng
Miss Sim is Research Officer of the East Asian Institute, Singapore. An Honours graduate of NUS Department of Economics and Statistics, she was formerly a senior officer with a government statutory board. Her research interests include macroeconomic development of China, Hong Kong–China economic integration, and reforms of Chinese state-owned enterprises.